For All Living Beings

For All Living Beings

A Guide to Buddhist Practice

Venerable Master Hsing Yun

Translated by Robert H. Smitheram

Published by Buddha's Light Publishing, Los Angeles

© 2010 Buddha's Light Publishing

By Venerable Master Hsing Yun
Translated by Robert H. Smitheram
Cover designed by Wilson Yau
Book designed by Wan Kah Ong and John Gill

Published by Buddha's Light Publishing
3456 S. Glenmark Drive,
Hacienda Heights, CA 91745, U.S.A.
Tel: (626) 923-5144
Fax: (626) 923-5145
E-mail: itc@blia.org
Website: www.blpusa.com

Printed in Taiwan.

Library of Congress Cataloging-in-Publication Data
Xingyun, da shi.
[Ren jian fo jiao de Jie ding hui. English]
For all living beings : a guide to Buddhist practice /
By Venerable Master Hsing Yun ; translated by Robert H. Smitheram.
p. cm.
ISBN 978-1-932293-40-1 (pbk.)
1. Buddhist monasticism and religious orders. 2. Monastic and religious life (Buddhism) I. Smitheram, Robert Hale. II. Title. III. Title: Guide to Buddhist practice.

BQ6083.X5613 2009
294.3'657—dc22

                                    2009031808

Contents

Part III: Wisdom

Acknowledgements

We received a lot of help from many people and we want to thank them for their efforts in making the publication of this book possible. We especially appreciate Venerable Tzu Jung, the Chief Executive of the Fo Guang Shan International Translation Center (F.G.S.I.T.C.), Venerable Hui Chi, Abbot of Hsi Lai Temple, and Venerable Yi Chao, Director of F.G.S.I.T.C. for their support and leadership; Robert H. Smitheram for his translation; Louvenia Ortega, John Gill, and Nathan Michon for their editing; Amanda Ling and Wan Kah Ong for preparing the manuscript for publication; and Wilson Yau for his cover design. Our appreciation also goes to everyone who has supported this project from its conception to its completion.

Acknowledgements

Introduction

When a young man enters the monastic order as a novice monk, he is called a *qinxi* (勤息) in Chinese. The second character, *xi*, means "quiet," and signifies that he will strive to quiet the three poisons of greed, anger, and ignorance in the mind. The first character, *qin*, means "diligence," and indicates that this person will diligently pursue what is called the "threefold training" in Buddhism: the cultivation of morality, meditative concentration, and wisdom. It is through the diligent pursuit of the threefold training that the poisons of greed, anger, and ignorance can be eliminated.

However, the threefold training does not belong only to monastics, but to all Buddhists everywhere. All great sages and bodhisattvas have undergone the threefold training, and it is a teaching that is shared by Mahayana, Vajrayana, and Theravada Buddhism alike.

The Buddhist scriptures themselves share a common structure with the threefold training. The *Tripitaka*, the core of the Buddhist canon, is divided into three divisions: *sutra, vinaya,* and *abhidharma*. The *sutras* contain the discourses of the Buddha and offer many teachings on developing meditative concentration; the *vinaya* details the discipline, rules, and morality for the Buddhist monastic order; and the *abhidharma* collects the analytical and commentarial tradition which focuses on the cultivation of wisdom. Anyone approaching the Buddhist teachings must bring the threefold training into their everyday thinking and living.

This book, *For All Living Beings*, is a guide to the threefold training. I have long advocated developing a "Humanistic Buddhism," and sought to integrate Buddhism into human life and our changing times. Nevertheless, Humanistic Buddhism should maintain traditional Buddhism at its core, which is why we continue to focus on the threefold training of morality, meditative concentration, and wisdom.

Chapter One

The Right Form for the Right Time
The Formulation of the Precepts

The Origin of the Precepts

M ORE THAN twenty-five hundred years ago, the Buddha entered final *nirvana* after teaching the Dharma for forty-nine years. Before he passed away the Buddha instructed his disciples to take the code of monastic conduct he had built up over the course of his life, the Buddhist precepts, and look to them as their teacher in his absence. Since then generations of followers have been able to learn the Dharma because of the preservation of these precepts. In fact, there is a Buddhist saying that "As long as the precepts abide, so too will the monastic order; and as long as the monastic order abides, so too will the Dharma." This is how Chinese Buddhism has endured over time: all those who wish to shave their heads and wear the robes of a monastic must be ordained through a formal ceremony of taking the precepts.

The Buddha formulated the monastic rules and precepts to regulate the monastic order and thus ensure that the right Dharma endures. Yet the precepts are not only observed by the monastic order. The precepts are the basis for all good deeds, and the cornerstone of all moral conduct.

One who observes the precepts is like a student who follows school regulations or a citizen who obeys the law. The difference is that school regulations and the law are restraints that come from something outside us. They are controls placed on us by other people, while Buddhist precepts are demands that we intentionally place upon ourselves as a form of self-control.

There are different sets of Buddhist precepts depending upon your gender and whether you are a monastic or a layperson. There are the five precepts, the eight precepts, and the ten precepts for laypeople; as well as the ten precepts of a novice monk or nun, the six precepts of a *siksamana*,[2] the 250 precepts of a fully ordained monk, and the 348 precepts of a fully ordained nun.

Each of these sets of precepts corresponds to a different type of person, and for this reason they are known as "specific precepts." In addition to the specific precepts, Mahayana Buddhism developed a set of precepts that apply to monastics and laypeople of both genders called the bodhisattva precepts. The bodhisattva precepts can be

 The Five Precepts

The five precepts form the basis of Buddhist morality for both laypeople and Buddhist monastics. The five precepts are:
1. To refrain from killing.
2. To refrain from stealing.
3. To refrain from sexual misconduct.
4. To refrain from lying.
5. To refrain from consuming intoxicants.

The Bodhisattva Precepts

The bodhisattva precepts are additional Mahayana precepts that focus on liberating ourselves and other living beings from suffering. They are primarily drawn from the *Brahma Net Sutra*, which lists forty-eight minor precepts that should be observed as well as ten major precepts to be kept at all times.

broken down into three categories: the precepts of proper conduct, the precepts for wholesome deeds, and the precepts for benefiting living beings. These bodhisattva precepts are for all people who wish to be awakened, and who vow to liberate living beings.

Another set of general precepts is contained in the *Verse of the Seven Ancient Buddhas*:

> *Do nothing that is unwholesome,*
> *Do all that is wholesome,*
> *Purify the mind.*
> *This is the teaching of all Buddhas.*

The Buddhist Monastic Rules

The origins and explanations of the Buddhist monastic rules are collected in a set of texts known as the *Vinaya*. The *Four Part Vinaya* records how the Buddha began formulating the monastic rules in the twelfth year after his enlightenment. At that time the monk Sudinna broke his renunciant vow of celibacy, thus prompting the Buddha to institute his first rule for the monastic order: that monastics were to refrain from sexual conduct.

The Buddha continued to formulate monastic rules as violations occurred. For example, the Theravada School has a rule against eating after noon. This rule stipulates that monastics must have their meals between morning and noon; all those who take their meals in the afternoon are said to have "eaten at an inappropriate time." The *Five Part Vinaya* records why the Buddha formulated this precept: The monk Kalodayin once entered the city of Rajagrha in the late afternoon to collect almsfood. As it was growing dark, a pregnant woman happened to catch a glimpse of Kalodayin and mistook him for a demon. The sudden shock was too much for her and she suffered a miscarriage. The Buddha felt that collecting alms at people's houses in the afternoon and evening created too many problems, so he created a rule that forbade monks from eating after noon.

The primary purpose of the Buddhist monastic rules is to prevent unwholesome conduct and wrongdoing. For example, the *Commentary on the Treatise in a Hundred Verses* states, "What is the intention behind the formulation of the monastic rules? To adopt what does no harm to all beings." On the other hand, the precepts also have the positive quality of benefiting others. *The Explanation of the Treatise on the Summary of Mahayana Doctrine* states, "In formulating the monastic rules the Tathagata's[3] intention was twofold: one was for the sake of sravakas[4] who liberate themselves, and the other was for bodhisattvas[5] who liberate others and liberate themselves."

The Chinese word for the Buddhist precepts is made up of two characters: *jie* (戒) and *lü* (律). The first character, *jie*, refers to a voluntary willingness to observe the precepts, while the character *lü* suggest an adherence to an external norm or standard. The various rules, regulations, and punishments for the monastic order are called *lü*, but when they are obeyed gladly and voluntarily they can be called *jie*.

Another explanation is that *jie* refers to those precepts in which the Buddha drew attention to the wrong actions of non-Buddhists as a way of instructing and admonishing his own disciples. These precepts apply to both monastics and laypeople, and are quite different from the monastic rules, *lü*, which were instituted as monastics committed specific offenses. There are no punishments attached to violating *jie*; rather, they are ways to improve ourselves through our own effort.

Regardless of how the precepts and monastic rules are defined, they were formulated to maintain the purity and harmony of the monastic order. The rules undoubtedly represent what should be the standard for daily life within the monastic order. Chapter twenty-two of the *Four Part Vinaya* lists ten benefits that come from observing the rules:

- The monastic order is supported by the rules.
- The monastics can be joyful.
- The monastics can be peaceful.
- Those without faith can find their faith.
- The faithful can deepen their faith.
- The obstinate can become cooperative.
- Those suffering from remorse can find peace.
- The outflows that are currently present can be removed.
- The outflows that will arise in the future can be removed.
- The right Dharma will last for a long time.

The first nine of these ten benefits guarantee the purity and harmony of the monastic order. Only the last one, that "the right Dharma will last for a long time," truly reflects the ultimate goal of the Buddha in instituting the monastic rules. This is because, as Master Taixu said, "The task of spreading the Buddhist teachings rests with the monastic community." When compared with some of the ordinary principles that exist to exert justice and maintain social order, the Buddhist precepts are more richly endowed with the Buddha's compassion to benefit living beings.

The Precepts Explained

When speaking of the Buddhist precepts, there are some who feel confused: Why do the laity have the five precepts, the bodhisattva precepts, the eight precepts, and so on, while the monastics have the monk's precepts, the nun's precepts, and the novice precepts? Why does Buddhism need such a large body of precepts?

Actually, the principle is quite simple. Just as students must study different curriculums at the primary, secondary, and collegiate levels, the different sets of Buddhist precepts are intended for different levels of development. The five precepts are the basis for proper conduct, the bodhisattva precepts are a practical application of the bodhisattva path to attain awakening while liberating living beings, and the eight precepts offer laypeople a convenient way to learn and experience the life of a monastic.

 The Eight Precepts

The eight precepts include the five precepts as well as additional precepts to refrain from eating at inappropriate times, attending performances of music and dance, wearing perfumes, or sleeping in luxurious beds. The eight precepts are typically taken by laypeople on retreat or when they wish to sample monastic life for a short time. Some lay Buddhists will take the eight precepts on certain special days throughout the year.

Another common question is why the five precepts contain a precept against consuming intoxicants. Is drinking alcohol really such a serious problem? To answer this question it is important to understand how the Buddha formulated the precepts. If an action is inherently unwholesome, the prohibitions against such behavior are known as "natural precepts." For example, killing, stealing, sexual misconduct, and lying are acts that violate natural law and forever change the moral character of the person who commits them. These behaviors are immoral whether or not Buddhism formulates a precept or the state enacts a law. The precepts prohibiting such actions are called natural precepts. If an action is not inherently unwholesome but allows for criticism or tempts one to act in an unwholesome way, the prohibitions against such behavior are known as "preclusive precepts." For example, drinking alcohol in and of itself is not evil, but doing so can easily cause you to lose your better judgment and kill, steal, engage in sexual misconduct, or lie. This is why the prohibition against intoxicants is listed after the four fundamental, major precepts.

The purpose of the preclusive precepts is to prevent outsiders from criticizing Buddhism, and they mostly deal with minor faults that society does not generally consider harmful. The preclusive precepts were formulated by the Buddha in response to particular circumstances and local conditions, usually being more minor in character than the natural precepts.

Besides the precept against intoxicants, other preclusive precepts include selling goods or digging up the ground to the injury of living beings. However, the Buddha made a special effort to include over-intoxication in the five precepts, because only by preventing such a transgression can the other precepts be kept safe.

The Buddha considered all aspects of the precepts and monastic rules fully and completely. The Buddhist precepts and monastic rules are not merely negative prohibitions against things; there is a permissive aspect as well. For example, if a bodhisattva who observes the precepts sees a robber preparing to kill living beings, the bodhisattva would end the life of that robber out of a sense of compassion. The bodhisattva would not be able to bear allowing the robber to create such negative karma that he would be reborn in hell. This is an example of when the precept against killing can be suspended.

The Buddhist Precepts and Law

There are some points of comparison between the Buddhist precepts and the laws of ordinary society. For example, some criminal acts recognized by the state such as murder, assault, robbery, rape, fraud, public drunkenness, and drug dealing are also found among the five precepts. However, there are major differences between the Buddhist teachings and secular law. According to the law, criminal intent is not necessarily evidence of guilt, for one can only be convicted of criminal conduct. In Buddhist practice, intention is sufficient for there to be a violation of the precepts. Buddhism places an extraordinary degree of emphasis upon the intention behind a transgression. Each precept and monastic rule includes details as to what is permitted, what is prohibited, what it means to obey it, and what it means to break it. Owing to differences in motive, manner, and result, breaking the same precept can be seen as different degrees of violation with varying forms of repentance. In this way the Buddhist precepts represent a more thorough approach to jurisprudence.

Skillful Means

The Buddhist teachings acknowledge that all people are conditioned in different ways. *Upaya*, or "skillful means," refers to the methods of any awakened teacher who adapts the Buddhist teachings so that a specific audience can learn. It also refers to bodhisattvas who use their infinite compassion and endless wisdom to liberate people from suffering, regardless of what conditions they find themselves in.

Alternatively, some actions which are considered crimes in the secular world may be seen as acceptable in Buddhism. For example, taking a human life is inherently a crime, but one can also take a life to save lives. Even the Buddha, while he was practicing the bodhisattva path in a previous life, killed one person so that he could save one hundred people. Thus we can see how the compassion of a bodhisattva expresses itself through the wisdom of skillful means.

The Precepts Today

Dynamically applying the spirit of the precepts to sometimes permit actions and sometimes forbid actions is a defining characteristic of the Mahayana approach. This approach is grounded in the Mahayana vows and the practice of compassion. This is the same attitude that Humanistic Buddhism has towards the Buddhist precepts. The fact that the Buddha's formulation of the precepts can be at times permissive or prohibitive also proves that the precepts are not unchangeable. They vary according to the particular circumstances when and where something happens, and depend upon who is involved.

The Buddha amended the monastic rules several times during his life to fit specific situations. For example, there was a rule that monks could only possess a single set of robes. When the Venerable Aniruddha wished to journey south to mediate a dispute, the Buddha stipulated that monks could possess more than one robe. On another occasion when some devotees offered an alms bowl to the Venerable Ananda, the Buddha relaxed the rules regarding the keeping of alms bowls. Clearly, the minor precepts governing the minutia of daily life could be changed as necessary, even in the time of the Buddha.

Regardless, even in the present day there are conservatives who hinder the innovation and development of Buddhism with the excuse, "The precepts that the Buddha laid down cannot be changed! Where the Buddha made no precept, no additions can be made!" This attitude has led to situations where different understandings of the rules and precepts have generated schisms within Buddhism.

On this point, I have always admired the wisdom of Chan Master Baizhang Huaihai who bypassed the rules and precepts, and instituted his *Rules of Purity for a Chan Temple* instead. At Fo Guang Shan, my own monastery in Taiwan, I developed a set of rules based upon the Buddhist precepts, Baizhang's rules, and the six points of reverent harmony. The six points of reverent harmony were formulated by the Buddha as a guide to creating peace and harmony in the monastic order. They are:

- "Maintain physical harmony by living together," which means not violating others.
- "Maintain verbal harmony by avoiding disputes," which means avoiding verbal arguments.

- "Maintain mental harmony by sharing happiness," which means having common spiritual goals and objectives.
- "Maintain moral harmony by observing the same precepts," which means that everyone is equal under the rules.
- "Maintain harmony in view by sharing the same understanding," which means establishing a consensus of thought.
- "Maintain economic harmony by sharing things equally," which means distributing benefits equally.

Similarly, Fo Guang Shan is organized around a set of ideals. Fo Guang Shan members are to remember that the monastery, the community, the devotees, and Buddhism itself come first while the individual comes second. Honor is to go to the Buddha, achievements belong to the community, benefit goes to the monastery, and merit and virtue go to the donors. Additionally, Fo Guang Shan has four main objectives:

- To propagate the Dharma through culture.
- To foster talent through education.
- To benefit society through charity.
- To purify the human mind through cultivation.

Fo Guang Shan emphasizes organization. When I was younger I realized that Buddhism's greatest flaw was its lack of organization. Buddhism had become like sand scattered in the wind, with everyone acting like a law unto themselves. Not only was there no uniformity in monastic attire, there was no strict system for joining the monastic order, taking ordination, receiving the precepts, or receiving a monastic education. Thus corruption became rampant.

For example, when I was a novice monk there was no functioning system governing the ordination ceremony. The situation was described by Master Yinguang as "the indiscriminate acceptance of disciples, the indiscriminate housing of wandering monks, and the indiscriminate transmission of the precepts."

This led to the complete breakdown of moral discipline. Teachers did not act like teachers and disciples did not act like disciples. The lack of a system created a class of people who acted like parasites and made their living off of Buddhism while contributing nothing. Without a good system, monastic property became privately owned. Even donations made to the monastery became the personal property of others, and were no longer used to spread the teaching and benefit living beings. That is why when I created my own monastery I took establishing a system quite seriously, and instituted twelve rules for the monastics at Fo Guang Shan to prevent these kinds of problems from developing:

- Do not miss shaving the head at the appropriate time.
- Do not stay overnight in the house of a layperson.
- Do not lend or borrow money from each other.
- Do not corrupt the monastic order.
- Do not accept your own disciples.
- Do not accumulate money for yourself.
- Do not establish your own temples.
- Do not keep your own devotees.
- Do not accept donations for yourself.
- Do not solicit donations for yourself.
- Do not deal in personal property.
- Do not make your own food or drink alone.

A system is like a flight of stairs that allows us to move upward, step by step, and make progress in the proper order. Only with a healthy system can there be a healthy monastic order, and only then can Buddhism be revitalized and go forward. The system itself must be instituted in accordance with the circumstances of time, place, and the people involved, for there is no room for dogmatism or conservatism. That being said, the truth of the Buddhist teachings should not be changed. There can be no doubt whatsoever on this point.

It is obvious that some of the Buddhist rules and precepts that were created more than twenty-five hundred years ago are no longer suitable for the demands of modern society. Though I would say that the fundamental precepts can be retained, some of the very minor precepts should be changed to meet modern needs or be otherwise adjusted to be flexible to the differences in local customs, climate, and geography. This is preferable to the blind observance of outmoded precedent. Without adjusting the precepts for novice monks in particular no progress is possible.

These are the areas we should face with a renewed sense of purpose. Only by recognizing the positive aspect of the Buddhist rules and precepts will we avoid forsaking the spirit of why the Buddha formulated the precepts in such an integrated and skillfully adaptive manner.

Chapter Two

The Human Quality of Morality
The Spirit of the Precepts

The Precepts and Freedom

W HEN MOST PEOPLE first hear about the Buddhist precepts, they may think they are just another set of rules to tell them all the things they cannot do and all the ways they will lose their freedom. This is not the case, for the simple spirit of the Buddhist precepts is that we should not violate each other. Just by not violating others we can respect one another and become free. For example, the first of the five precepts is to abstain from killing, which means to not violate the life of others. To abstain from stealing is to not violate the property of others. To abstain from sexual misconduct is to not violate the body of others. To abstain from lying is to not violate the reputation of others. To abstain from intoxicants is to not impair your judgment so as to avoid violating others.

When we do not violate others and, by extension, respect one another, we can enjoy freedom. If we look into why people get locked up in prison and lose their freedom we can see that it is usually as a result of breaking the five precepts. Murder and assault are violations of the precept against killing; stealing, embezzlement, extortion, robbery, and kidnapping are violations of the precept against stealing; rape, human trafficking, bigamy, and lewd behavior are violations of the precept against sexual misconduct; defamation, false testimony, and threats of violence are violations of the precept against lying; and drug dealing, drug addiction, drug trafficking, and alcohol abuse are violations of the precept against intoxicants.

Violating the five precepts can lead to imprisonment and a loss of freedom. By observing the precepts we also obey secular law, and it is by observing the precepts that we can become free. The laws of the state will not excuse someone who breaks the precepts and commits an illegal act, and the law of karma will continue to affect him. Observing the precepts should not be seen as more control. Those who undertake, follow, and truly understand the precepts are the ones who enjoy true freedom.

In Buddhism, taking refuge in the Triple Gem of the Buddha, Dharma, and Sangha marks the beginning of Buddhist practice, while undertaking and observing the precepts is the application of this faith. After taking refuge in the Triple Gem, all Buddhist

Karma

Karma is the Buddhist concept of cause and effect. Everything we do, say, and think acts as a cause that will have an effect on this current life or in a future life. Harmful actions will create negative results, and helpful actions create positive results. The results of karma are not imposed on us by some sort of deity, but occur due to the natural Law of Cause and Effect.

The Triple Gem

In all Buddhist cultures the beginning of the Buddhist path is to take refuge in the Triple Gem of the *Buddha, Dharma,* and *Sangha.* Taking refuge in the Buddha refers not only to taking refuge in the Buddha as a teacher, but in awakening itself. Taking refuge in the Dharma means to accept the Buddha's teachings and put them into practice. Taking refuge in the Sangha means to take refuge in the monastic order.

followers should take the next step and aspire to undertake the precepts. Undertaking the precepts is a kind of aspiration that, once it has been made, will make any corrupt or divergent thought run away and hide. This is because the precepts are the basis for all wholesome conduct. The *Treatise on the Perfection of Great Wisdom* [*Mahaprajnaparamita Sastra*] states:

> *In the face of a terrible disease,*
> *the precepts are good medicine;*
> *Amidst great fear,*
> *the precepts are a secure defense;*
> *Amidst death's shadow,*
> *the precepts are a bright lamp;*
> *Along a perilous road,*
> *the precepts are a bridge to safety;*
> *In deadly waters, the precepts are a great ship.*

Being able to undertake and observe the precepts will naturally give you great strength and great merit. However, it is important that we have the correct knowledge and view of the spirit of the precepts. This is even more important than observing the precepts.

Wrong View

Breaking the precepts is a transgression—an error in one's behavior that can be corrected through repentance and reform. Wrong view, on the other hand, is a misunderstanding of the truth and a more fundamental error in one's thinking. Someone who holds a wrong view will not be able to understand, comprehend, or accept the Buddha's teachings, and will thus be forever disconnected from the Buddhist path. One can easily repent and reform after breaking the precepts, but this is not the case for one who holds wrong views.

One example of a wrong view is the view that "It is next to impossible to undertake the precepts without breaking them, but by not undertaking the precepts I no longer need to worry about the negative karma from breaking them." Actually, the negative karma from breaking the precepts one has undertaken is somewhat small. This is because one has a sense of regret and repents. Such people still have a chance to be liberated. Those who have not undertaken the precepts break them without a sense of remorse, and thus their negative karma is all the more severe since they do not correct their behavior. Such people will be reborn as animals, hungry ghosts, or in hell.

Breaking the precepts is nothing to be ashamed of since, as long as you sincerely repent, you can still have hope for the next life. On the other hand, someone who holds a wrong view is like a person with an incurable disease that no medicine can treat.

In Buddhism, it is said that there are five kinds of view that cloud understanding: views of the body, extreme views, evil views, views that attach to wrong views as truth, and views attached to immorality. All of these views are sources of affliction and obstruct us on the path. For this reason, it is important that anyone learning the Buddhist teachings first develop right knowledge and understanding. They must know that, when undertaking the precepts, they will have a standard of conduct to follow. They must understand self-restraint, and know that if the precepts are broken, repentance is still possible. We should not fear the precepts, for it is only by means of the precepts that we can have peace, security, and protection.

Proscriptive Observance and Prescriptive Observance

The Buddhist precepts require both proscriptive observance and prescriptive observance. For example, the line "Do nothing that is unwholesome" from the *Verse of the Seven Ancient Buddhas* is proscriptive observance. The next line, "Do all that is wholesome," is prescriptive observance. When one refrains from unwholesome deeds that are illegal or immoral, that is observing the precepts, while engaging in such behavior would be breaking the precepts. Similarly, engaging in wholesome deeds that benefit others is observing the precepts, while any evasion or omission is breaking the precepts. This shows how the Buddhist precepts not only cover the negative aspect of stopping wrongdoing, but also include the positive encouragement to do good. Therefore, besides the specific precepts for the different classes of disciples that constitute the negative prohibition against wrongdoing, there are also the bodhisattva precepts that serve as a positive encouragement to do good.

As mentioned previously, there are three categories of bodhisattva precepts:

1. The precepts for proper conduct are the various Buddhist rules and precepts instituted to prevent wrongdoing.
2. The precepts for wholesome deeds constitute a vow to practice all wholesome deeds.

3. The precepts for benefiting sentient beings are a commitment to benefit all sentient beings.

Chapter four of the *Sutra on Bodhisattva Stages* [*Bodhisattvabhumi Sutra*] lists eleven methods to benefit living beings:

1. When sentient beings are engaged in beneficial activities, join and support them.
2. Support sentient beings who are sick, those who are not yet sick though still suffer and those who treat the sick.
3. Expound the mundane teachings and the supramundane teachings to all sentient beings, and employ skillful means so that they will attain wisdom.
4. Treat others' kindness with gratitude.
5. Rescue sentient beings from their fears and liberate them from their difficulties, so that they turn away from worry and distress.
6. Seeing that sentient beings are poor and needy, bestow upon them all that they need.
7. Take refuge in those who are complete in virtue and use the right Dharma to gather the people.
8. First comfort people through speech, visit them from time to time, give them food and drink, and speak good words to them. In this way, those who are peaceful will become better and those who are not peaceful will be able to turn away from their anxieties.
9. Praise those who have virtuous conduct and treat them well.
10. Kindly and compassionately scold those who have unwholesome conduct so that they will repent and change their ways.
11. Use supernatural powers to show people the lower realms so that sentient beings will fear wrongdoing, practice the Dharma

joyfully, have faith, and keep in mind that the Dharma is rare in this world.

The three categories of the bodhisattva precepts show how the Buddhist precepts are not merely a negative prohibition against all unwholesome deeds, but also a positive injunction to do all wholesome deeds. The goal of the precepts is to purify yourself and benefit others. This is why not doing something you should do is also considered breaking the precepts. The Buddhist precepts are wonderful in their breadth and simplicity, and they show the true spirit of morality that those who practice the bodhisattva path should master.

Humanizing the Precepts

There are many Buddhist precepts which are difficult to observe in modern society. For example, the ten precepts for novice monks and nuns contain a precept against carrying money, a precept against attending performances of music or dance, and a precept against sleeping in a high and wide bed.

There are many issues facing modern Buddhism. Japanese Buddhism has married clergy and hereditary inheritance of temples. Tibetan Buddhist monastics can eat meat on certain occasions. Some Buddhist temples use modern ceremonial items made from animal hides, to say nothing of the debate about vegetarian food which is modeled and named after meat dishes. How are we supposed to deal with all of that?

There is no need to hold on to the Buddhist rules and precepts in a formal and mechanical way. It is more important to emphasize the spirit, meaning, and humanistic quality of the precepts. Ordination in Chinese Mahayana Buddhism expresses the spirit of the precepts well, and is done through the "Triple Platform Full Ordination Ceremony." The three platforms mentioned in the ceremony refer to different sets of precepts: the first platform is for the novice precepts which support the observance of proper conduct, the second platform is for the monastic precepts which support the practice of wholesome deeds, and the third platform is for the bodhisattva precepts which benefit living beings. It is because these three categories of precepts are fully established that Mahayana Buddhism has been able to develop as it has. This is a unique characteristic of the rules and precepts of Humanistic Buddhism.

The Buddhist precepts should enhance our lives and make the future brighter. In the past, the Buddhist precepts put too much emphasis on the negative sanctions against wrongdoing. Any mention of the precepts meant a lot of "don't do this" and "don't do that." Besides the examples previously cited there are also rules that prohibit monastics from giving money or goods to lay devotees, keep laypeople from listening to the recitation of the monastic rules, and stipulate that monks must keep their distance from women.

The five precepts are the basis of human morality. However, in the past the human aspect of the precepts was undermined. People would quote passages from the *Brahma Net Sutra* [*Brahmajala Sutra*] like "touching wine with your hand will deprive you of hands for five hundred lifetimes." The excessive use of intimidation and threats had the opposite effect and diminished their persuasive power. As a result, those who were interested in Buddhism would step back in hesitation. In particular the "Eight Precepts of Respect," a set of stringent precepts for Buddhist nuns, has hindered many well-qualified women from joining the monastic order for thousands of years. These modern times definitely need more ethical guidance, and thus we should humanize the Buddhist precepts.

To humanize the Buddhist precepts we should retain the negative constraints on the body and mind to refrain from wrongdoing, but we should also emphasize the positive cultivation of good conduct and good deeds in all areas. We should develop the spirit of service and altruism found in the bodhisattva precepts to benefit both ourselves and others. It is no longer appropriate for the modern Buddhist world to make demands upon modern people based on the social conditions of the Buddha's time. Though the Buddha was an expert in the monastic rules and precepts, he formulated them according to the customs, culture, and people in India at that time. However, things have changed, and many precepts no longer fit with the progress that has been made over the centuries.

One such example is the monastic rule to wear the robe on one side, so that it exposes the right shoulder. India has a tropical climate, but compelling people who live in a colder climate to observe this precept is not reasonable. Another example is the monastic rule against carrying money. Ancient India did not use currency the way we do today—modern people cannot feed, clothe, shelter, or transport themselves without money.

Another monastic rule that needs to be reconsidered is the rule that monks should have no contact with women. To ensure the strength of the monastic order the Buddha did establish such strict rules and precepts; but in an age when the two sexes have equal rights men and women frequently come in contact with each other. For example, seating during meetings is on a first come, first serve basis; and when boarding public transportation, both men and women line up together. As long as there is a clear distinction between what is public and what is private, it is normal, ordinary social interaction for modern men and women to meet each other.

The various precepts to prevent criticism should also be re-examined. These precepts are sometimes carried to an extreme, resulting in so much fear of being critiqued that one cannot do anything. Since too much scrutiny is exercised the Buddhist teachings will be deprived of their original sense of purpose and their engagement to benefit living beings, such that Buddhism itself loses its power to transform in the modern age.

This is why I believe that the principles for formulating the precepts must be sensible and rational, and that they must respect human feelings and human nature. As mentioned earlier, Chan Master Baizhang Huaihai bypassed the monastic rules and instituted his *Rules of Purity for a Chan Temple* instead. In this modern era Humanistic Buddhism is adapting to current trends as well. The traditional monastic rules and precepts that are appropriate to the given situation should be respected, while separate rules should be formulated for living in modern society. This shows that Buddhism is contemporary while conforming to the spirit of the Buddha's formulation of the precepts at the same time.

The various regional forms of Buddhism should have a thorough understanding of the spirit and purpose of the monastic rules and precepts. Simply relying upon rules and precepts as something fixed and immutable since the Buddha's time will limit the development of Buddhism. It is only through the mutual respect of each nation's traditions, popular sentiments, and social customs that we can reach a consensus and advance the unity and development of world Buddhism.

The Buddhist precepts are about self-cultivation and benefiting others. In fact, it is said that when one perfects what it means to

> ### What is Humanistic Buddhism?
>
> Humanistic Buddhism is nothing new, but instead represents a return to the principles laid down by the Buddha. Humanistic Buddhism recognizes that the Buddha lived in the human world and taught the Dharma in the human world, and that Buddhism should be for human beings. Humanistic Buddhism is Buddhism that is timeless, joyful, altruistic, and life-affirming.

be human, Buddhahood is attained. From the outward forms of cultivation and purification to the unwavering thoughts within the mind, the precepts operate on many different levels. The times have changed, and many minor precepts are no longer applicable. Because of this, and because of the moral corruption of our times, it is important to employ the fundamental spirit of the precepts, like the non-violation of others, while promoting the five precepts and the bodhisattva vows. This is the only way to correct our corrupt morality and disorderly society.

The only way to bring about the betterment of living beings is to demand that our morals meet standards that are humanistic, life-affirming, and modern. We must establish a Humanistic Buddhism which accepts and upholds the precepts of the bodhisattva path that benefits both ourselves and others and integrates the Buddhist teachings of the Noble Eightfold Path, the four means of embracing, and the six perfections into the precepts. After all, the Noble Eightfold Path, the four means of embracing, and the six perfections are indeed the precepts themselves, for only that which supports the betterment of living beings can truly be called the Buddhist precepts.

Chapter Three

Living Well

The Application of the Precepts

Applying the Precepts

THE *Avatamsaka Sutra* states, "The precepts are the supreme basis for *bodhi* that nurtures all wholesome roots." The precepts are the life force of the Buddhist teachings, and are the source that all Buddhas draw upon to transform the world. The Buddha said that all living beings have Buddha nature, but even though Buddha nature is present we must observe the precepts for it to manifest itself. That is why the *Sutra of Teachings Bequeathed by the Buddha* [*Fo Yijiao Jing*] says, "If one can observe the precepts purely, then one will obtain all wholesome Dharmas; if the precepts are impure, all wholesome virtues will not arise."

Observing the precepts is the foundation for cultivating all good teachings and is the basis for all Buddhist practice. However, it is not enough just to recite the precepts; they must be put into practice. As long as we do good deeds, speak good words, and keep good thoughts in our normal, everyday lives we can purify

Buddha Nature

Buddha nature is the intrinsic quality of awakening that lies in every living being. Though this quality may not be fully realized in most people, the fact that all living beings have Buddha nature means that we all have the potential to become Buddhas.

our karma. In this way, we can put into practice the verse, "Do nothing that is unwholesome, do all that is wholesome, and purify the mind." If we can see the workings of the law of karma in everything we do, that is practicing the precepts.

The Buddhist precepts are meant for us to regulate ourselves, not to make demands of others. The spirit of the precepts lies in observing them with purity, having the aspiration for enlightenment, and benefiting living beings. To truly practice the precepts we must observe all three categories of the bodhisattva precepts to liberate all living beings.

Without the aspiration to seek enlightenment while benefiting living beings, one cannot be called a bodhisattva. Though the bodhisattva precepts are characterized by the ten major precepts against killing, stealing, sexual conduct, lying, consuming intoxicants, criticizing others, praising oneself and slandering others, covetousness, unrepentant anger, and slandering the Triple Gem, and the forty-eight minor precepts, their basic spirit is the aspiration to seek enlightenment. The aspiration for enlightenment is the essence of the bodhisattva precepts, and forgetting this aspiration would be a violation of the essential spirit of the bodhisattva precepts.

Most Buddhists spend their time meditating, reciting the name of Amitabha Buddha, and correcting their bodies and minds. If they have extra time, they should devote it to volunteer work, community service, or making donations to relieve poverty and help the needy. They can also assist in publishing Buddhist books, spreading the Buddhist teachings, or even participate in cultural or educational activities like establishing Buddhist schools. To practice the three categories of the bodhisattva precepts we must practically apply the bodhisattva path.

Observing the precepts is the concrete manifestation of compassion and the bodhisattva path. This is epitomized by the Confucian dictum, "Do not do unto others what you would not wish done unto you." Because of this, most Chinese Buddhists practice some form of vegetarianism. Some will have a vegetarian meal at noon and then observe a fast on the first and fifteen days of the lunar month. Others will eat vegetarian porridge in the morning. While such practices are not the strictest, these people do at least have the resolve to have a vegetarian meal when those special days occur.

Buddhists do not have a monopoly on vegetarianism, but the Buddhist practice of vegetarianism is special in that it serves as a way to foster compassion and a respect for life. Nothing in this world is more cruel or barbaric than killing living beings. Even a single ant, cockroach, fly, or mosquito is a living being, and they treasure their lives. However, when most people see an ant or a mosquito they kill them with a single swat of their hands or stomp them to death with their feet. Even though there are times when such insects become a nuisance in our lives, we should drive them away or take preventative steps beforehand. We cannot simply kill them, for their crimes do not warrant death. Taking their lives so suddenly is much too harsh.

While observing the Buddhist precepts may have its basis in faith, at their core the precepts are based upon a compassionate mind. When we practice the five precepts, we are able to offer others fearlessness. This is because, when one practices the precepts with purity, others need not fear that they will be violated in any way. This is why the five precepts are also sometimes called the "five great offerings."

The Benefits of Practicing the Precepts

The five precepts are the fundamental precepts of Buddhism. Though there are different sets of Buddhist precepts for monastics and laypeople, all the various precepts are based on the five precepts. When you observe and practice the five precepts not only will you be protected by the twenty-five Dharma guardians,[6] you benefit both yourself and others. For example, in the case of the precept against killing you become more compassionate while the others do not lose their life. For the precept against stealing you do not ruin your moral character and others do not lose their wealth. For the precept against sexual misconduct your family life remains harmonious and others do not lose their honor. For the precept against lying, you are seen as trustworthy and others are spared from praise or blame. For the precept against intoxicants you do not damage your own wisdom and others are spared from any harm.

Going beyond the letter of the precepts grants us even more benefit. When we go beyond not killing and protect others we will naturally be healthy and have longevity. When we go beyond not stealing and practice generosity we will become rich and honored. When we go beyond not engaging in sexual misconduct and respect the good name of others our family life will naturally become harmonious. When we go beyond not lying and praise others we will naturally obtain prestige and distinction. When we go beyond not consuming intoxicants and turn away completely from the temptation of drugs we will naturally have a healthy body and a clear mind.

By practicing the five precepts we can be free from fear and suffering. We can obtain freedom, peace, harmony, and happiness in this life. Additionally, we can avoid rebirth in the lower realms and enjoy rebirth as a human being or in heaven, ultimately attaining Buddhahood. It is like planting a seed in a field of merit. Though there should be no expectation of reward, many benefits will naturally accrue and one will enjoy inexhaustible merit and good karmic results.

In general, all people hope to live a long life, be wealthy and respected, and have a happy family life with many children. If you pray to the Buddha and bodhisattvas and ask for these things, yet reject the practice of the five precepts, how do you expect to get them? How can you get the result without the cause? When viewed negatively, observing the five precepts does appear to be a form of restraint. Yet when they are viewed positively, observing the precepts is like finding a light within darkness, or like a poor man finding a precious jewel. Indeed, the are unlimited benefits.

Right Livelihood

Though observing the five precepts brings many benefits, modern people often decide not to take them because they find their jobs make it impossible to keep them. For example, someone who works in a fabric store may encounter a customer who looks over some cloth and asks, "Will the colors on this fabric fade?" If the shopkeeper were to answer truthfully there would certainly be no sale. This is why shopkeepers sometimes lie out of expediency. Likewise, there are farmers who will say that, "We plant fields and tend fruit trees, and for the sake of a good harvest we simply must use pesticides. How could we dare undertake the precepts?"

Practicing the precepts does not require that they never be broken, and trying to observe the precepts in today's world is certainly no easy task. There are many seaside communities that make their living by fishing. According to the Noble Eightfold Path, such people engage in wrong action and wrong livelihood, so how can they follow the Buddhist path and undertake the precepts?

This question reminds me of a visit I made to Little Liouchiou Island. When the Buddha's Light International Association was just getting started there was a chapter on the island, and I was invited to attend one of its conferences. The president of the chapter told me, "The residents of our island make their living mostly from fishing, and this conflicts with the Buddhist precept against killing. But if everyone observed the precept against killing, we'd have nothing to eat, so it's hard to promote Buddhism here."

I told him that, though Buddhism teaches us not to kill, distinctions are still made based on severity. When it comes to the precept against killing, there is the distinction between the act of killing and the intention to kill. When you go fishing, you do so to maintain your life—there is no thought of killing. It is similar

The Buddha's Light International Association

The Buddha's Light International Association is a lay Buddhist organization founded in 1992 by Venerable Master Hsing Yun as a way for laypeople to become involved in propagating Humanistic Buddhism. The BLIA serves a variety of social, religious, and charitable functions, and has more than 150 chapters all over the world.

to cremating the corpse after someone dies. The flames will not only kill the parasites in the corpse, but the parasites in the wood will die too! Yet we do not mean to kill anyone, and there was no intention to kill. Even if the precepts are broken in such cases, it is a minor violation. Moreover, the situation can still be salvaged as long as one feels sincere remorse.

Buddhism is a religion based on human beings, and though it values the life of even the smallest creature, we actually destroy numerous lives every day without thinking about or realizing it. For example, when we breathe, does the air not contain microorganisms? Aren't there small creatures in our food and drink? How can we possibly avoid harming the tiny life that depends upon our bodies when the body itself is treated with medicine, undergoes operations, is cremated, or buried in the ground? In each of those moments we had no intention to kill. Even though there may be some acts of killing as we cultivate ourselves spiritually, we must not generate the mental karma of killing living beings. Even though our actions harm small organisms, we must feel ashamed for so carelessly destroying life and deeply repent over it. This is the spirit of the Buddhist precepts.

It is commonly said, "Taking the precepts is easy, observing them is hard." However, it is important to note that just because something is hard does not mean that we should completely avoid it. The five precepts can be taken together or they can be taken in steps. As stated in the *Treatise on the Perfection of Great Wisdom* [*Mahaprajnaparamita Sastra*]:

> *There are five precepts, starting with the no killing and ending with no intoxicants. If one can undertake one precept, it is called "one step."*

> *If one can undertake two or three precepts, it is called "fewer steps." If one can undertake four precepts, it is called "more steps." Undertaking all five precepts is called "full steps." As to which one to take among these steps, one can choose as one wishes.*

This shows that laypeople can select the one or two precepts that are easy for them to observe according to their own circumstances, and later practice the precepts more diligently with three or four, until they gradually reach the full five precepts. Even if someone is engaged in wrong livelihood, once committed to the Buddhist path he can take a few steps by undertaking the precepts in a way that is convenient. As opportunities arise and karmic conditions slowly change over time, he will discover that there are thousands of other professions in this world. If you do not engage in this line of work, you can be employed in another one. It is certainly not necessary to make a living through killing, and you certainly do not need to work in any profession that harms people. It is possible to change your job and still have what you need to live.

Besides providing the necessities of life, work can be the best form of practice. With our jobs we can make donations, perform service, and create connections for a positive future. Not only should we engage in a proper profession, we must also have professional ethics.

When we work, we should understand the law of karma. Never use one's public station to engage in corruption, commit fraud, seek private gain at the public's expense, profit from forced seizures, or benefit from intimidation or enticements. Everything that is gained should be returned to the public in total.

We must possess the power of patience. Do not complain when tasked with responsibilities and do not blame others when difficulties arise. We must work hard without complaint, for everything should be seen as a matter of course. Only by possessing the power of patience can one be responsible and do the job well.

We should be conscientious in our work, bear responsibilities earnestly and take pleasure in doing so. When something happens, we should not shift it to others, for one should not enjoy abusing other people. We should make things easier for others and serve them.

We should remember to be grateful for everything: be thankful that your boss has given you a job and be thankful that your coworkers and subordinates have assisted in your work. With a grateful heart it is possible to do all things happily, no matter how busy or tired you may be.

The true meaning of the Buddhist precepts lies in integrating them into our lives so that in all matters and interactions with other people we can overcome our selfishness, return to propriety, and cultivate ourselves. We should follow the Buddhist teachings and precepts in every deed, so that we avoid violating each other, and treat one another with tolerance and respect. This is the "proscriptive observance" of the precepts. To take the next step we must grant others faith and joy as well as help one another. This is the "prescriptive observance" of the precepts, and it is the best model for putting the precepts of Humanistic Buddhism into practice.

Chapter Four

Into the Everyday
Fulfilling the Precepts

Beyond Rules and Regulations

THROUGHOUT HUMAN HISTORY, the greatest accomplishments have come from religion, and the greatest works of art, theatre, and literature have been inspired by religion. Religion enabled the glorious achievements of human civilization and has ennobled the innate character of humanity. Religion has been able to do this because of its creation of rules, precepts, and systems of morality.

All religions have their rules and precepts that must be followed. The Buddhist precepts are special because they are mostly concerned with the cultivation of morality. For a Buddhist, the only way to truly respect the Buddha is by perfecting his or her human character. We can only attain inner wisdom and realize the highest levels of truth after we are good and moral people. That is why, after taking refuge in the Triple Gem, all Buddhists should request to undertake the precepts. The precepts serve as the foundation for learning Buddhism and being a moral person.

Similes on the Precepts

- The precepts are like a good teacher who guides our direction in life.
- The precepts are like a splash of water that washes away the dirt and grime of our afflictions.
- The precepts are like a beacon of light that makes our future bright.
- The precepts are like a magic sword that cuts away greed and desire.
- The precepts are like a ferry that delivers us to the other shore of *nirvana*.

Compassion is the spirit of the Buddhist precepts. We can see the importance of compassion by looking at the Buddha himself. While the Buddha was practicing the bodhisattva path in his many past lives he once cut off a piece of his own flesh to feed an eagle. On another occasion he sacrificed his own body to feed a tiger. In the same way, there are many stories of young novices who would rather give their lives to keep the precepts than to live an ignoble life by breaking them. Today Buddhist practitioners continue to develop their compassion by keeping the teachings, keeping the precepts, keeping their promises, and keeping the faith.

The Buddhist precepts are like the pleasant fragrance of a lotus flower. When someone practices the precepts purely the fragrance of the precepts pervades the whole world, and that person is praised everywhere he goes. The *Sutra on the Fragrance of the Precepts* [*Jie xiang jing*] says, "The fragrances of all the flowers and fruits in the world, even sandalwood and musk, cannot be sensed everywhere. Only the fragrance of the precepts pervades the whole universe."

The Buddha was an enlightened being who observed moral principles with diligence and purity. Not only did he hold himself to a strict moral code, he also formulated a host of rules and precepts, such as the five precepts and the bodhisattva precepts, as a way to transform the minds and bodies of his disciples. Upali, one of the Buddha's ten great disciples, was known for his great discipline and knowledge of the monastic precepts. Master Daoxun, the founder of the Nanshan Vinaya School, was so diligent in his observance of the precepts that he was said to possess "the immaculate fragrance of the precepts, and the extraordinary clarity of meditative concentration."

Buddhist morality has many different facets, each of which helps to improve our lives. The five precepts and the ten wholesome actions help us develop a sound human character, the conduct of Buddhist sages helps elevate our morality, and the bodhisattva's

The Ten Wholesome Actions

The ten wholesome actions are a more detailed version of the five precepts, and show us how to act wholesomely with our body, speech, and mind. They are:

1. To refrain from killing.
2. To refrain from stealing.
3. To refrain from sexual misconduct.
4. To refrain from lying.
5. To refrain from duplicitous speech.
6. To refrain from harsh speech.
7. To refrain from flattery.
8. To refrain from greed.
9. To refrain from anger.
10. To refrain from ignorance.

wisdom of emptiness helps us understand the mind and see our nature. Whatever comes from a compassionate mind and neither contradicts secular law nor the gets in the way of benefiting all living beings can lead us to fulfill our human character and become enlightened.

Buddhist morality goes far beyond the precepts. Such qualities as connecting with others through generosity, forgetting others' past misdeeds, having remorse, watching over the six sense organs, and being a good friend are part of Buddhist morality as well. Being grateful for the kindness we receive is also part of Buddhist morality, for we should be grateful for the kindness offered to us by our parents, other living beings, our country, and the Triple Gem. We should apply skillful means, bring benefit and happiness to all living beings, give to everyone universally, and spread the teachings far and wide. We should be tolerant, gentle, mindful, and always have kind words for others. All of this is part of Buddhist morality.

We should each strive to have the great kindness, great compassion, great wisdom, and great practice of the Buddhas and bodhisattvas. We should aspire to become enlightened, and vow to liberate all living beings, even those who have done unspeakably terrible things like murder their parents, kill an arhat,[7] injure a Buddha, or destroy the harmony of the monastic order. This is the perfection of Buddhist morality, and the way to practice the bodhisattva precepts.

The Mission of Humanistic Buddhism

Sun Yat-sen, the father of modern China, once said, "Buddhism is the mother of philosophy and the benevolence that saves the world. A study of Buddhist teaching can compensate for the one-sidedness of science." Not only does Buddhism compensate for the one-sidedness of science, it can also compensate for the incompleteness of law. The law imposes sanctions for what has already happened, while the Buddhist teachings are designed to prevent trouble before it happens. As long as the headwaters of a river are clear, its outlet will naturally be free of pollution. By engaging in the spiritual transformation of society, Buddhism works to purify the headwaters of humanity.

As trouble becomes rampant throughout society, there are those who may say that a chaotic world demands harsh punishment. In reality, legal sanctions are only intimidating for a short time; they cannot put an end to criminal behavior forever. The Buddhist precepts have the ability to reform society by teaching us to be compassionate, respect life, support all living beings, and be disciplined as well as instilling the importance of the Law of Cause and Effect and the power of repentance. These reforms are the mission of Humanistic Buddhism.

Humanistic Buddhism must concern itself with these social problems. To try to give ordinary people a way to improve their own personal morality, I have worked with the Buddha's Light International Association for many years to create programs to address the moral problems of our society. One of these was the "Seven Admonitions Campaign," the seven admonitions are:

- The admonition against smoking and drugs
- The admonition against visiting brothels
- The admonition against violence
- The admonition against stealing
- The admonition against gambling
- The admonition against alcohol abuse
- The admonition against harsh speech

The seven admonitions show us concrete ways that we can bring the five precepts into our lives by staying away from smoking, drugs, prostitution, violence, and other vices. A similar campaign, called the "Three Benevolent Acts Campaign," consisted of the following:

- Do good deeds
- Speak good words
- Keep good thoughts

They may seem simple, but the three benevolent acts are an easy way to practice the Buddhist teachings. Karma is created through how we act, how we speak, and how we think. By doing good deeds, we change our harmful actions into the helpful actions of a Buddha. By speaking good words, we transform harsh and jealous speech into the gentle speech of a Buddha. By keeping good thoughts we eliminate thoughts that are ignorant, negative, or full of confusion and instead have the compassionate and wise thoughts of a Buddha. The Three Benevolent Acts campaign is really a campaign for all of us to purify our karma and become Buddhas, one step at a time.

These campaigns coincided with another campaign called the "Reclaim Our Minds Campaign." The body is like a castle, and the mind is like a king, ruling over our five senses. For this reason we must make sure we are in charge of the mind. This campaign was an initiative for all BLIA members to respect life, care for society, reclaim our minds and use them to do good. We must be able to reclaim the noble qualities of the mind, and use them to benefit ourselves and others.

The BLIA has been successful over the years, gaining many members and opening up chapters all over the world. As a lay organization it has been able to further the mission of Humanistic Buddhism and spread Buddhism to the people. However, like all Buddhist organizations, the BLIA is made up of human beings and there will be disagreements.

To try to prevent these problems, when the BLIA was founded the "Seven Rules for Eliminating Conflict" were created to resolve disputes. The rules were based on the Buddhist teachings, and have worked well, allowing the BLIA to spend its time helping others rather than engaging in petty in-fighting. The seven rules are as follows:

1. Both parties involved in a dispute are given the opportunity to state their case and the leaders of the BLIA chapter will pass judgment on it.
2. Anyone accused of wrongdoing is given the opportunity to state whether the accusation is true or not. If the accused person says that the accusations are false, that is okay. That person need only answer to the Triple Gem and their own conscience. There is no need to persist in accusing that person.
3. If someone is not in a normal, healthy state of mind, it is important to wait until that person's mind returns to normal before going any further. When things are back to normal, ask that person to repent before a Buddha statue.
4. If someone has confessed to wrongdoing they should make amends with the person who they wronged or to the Buddha.
5. If someone's words and actions are clearly contradictory, yet that person will not admit fault and expresses no remorse for his behavior, his membership in the BLIA will be suspended and he will not be allowed to hold any leadership position or receive any kind of award in the future.

6.   If two parties argue with one another endlessly and there is no
     resolution in sight, a group of five to seven virtuous monastics
     will be gathered to try to resolve the incident. Anyone who
     goes against the majority decision of the group is expelled
     from the association.
7.   If both parties admit fault, they may bow to one another to
     restore their standing.

Transformed by the Precepts

The Buddhist precepts are here to protect us from wrongdoing,
lead us away from what is bad, and towards what is good. Vinaya
Master Daoxuan of the Tang dynasty composed the *Simplified and
Amended Handbook of the Four-Part Vinaya* [*Sifenlü Shanfan
Buque Xingshi Chao*], in which he analyzed the precepts in terms
of their "rules," "essence," "practice," and "characteristics." When one
puts the actual rules of the precepts into practice, the body and
mind receive the essence of the precepts. When this happens, that
essence is expressed through the practice of being pure in body,
speech, and mind.

Those who practice the precepts will gain the characteristics
of the precepts and radiate them outwards. Such people will have
a naturally majestic and dignified bearing and always act in
a moral way. Practicing the precepts can purify our bodies and
minds, improve our morality, refine our character, and reveal our
Buddha nature. By practicing the precepts we can be sure that our
motivation will not fail us, and that we will be endowed with all
the merits of practicing the precepts. The precepts are, quite clearly,
essential to our lives.

Buddhism is a religion that advocates equality. In Buddhism it
is said that everyone can become a Buddha. In fact, we should not

disrespect anyone, for they too will one day become a Buddha. It is by observing the precepts that this unique quality is created and refined, until we reach the goal of respecting human rights and the right to life. We must reach this goal to truly elevate the moral character of all human beings.

It is by applying the five precepts, the ten wholesome actions, and the three categories of bodhisattva precepts that it becomes possible to fulfill our human character, attain enlightenment, benefit all, and liberate ourselves and others. This is why the Buddhist precepts are so admirable, and why encouraging all to undertake and practice them is the ultimate goal of Humanistic Buddhist Morality.

Chapter Five

The World of Chan
The Origins of Meditative Concentration

The Power of Meditative Concentration

WHEN WE TALK about meditation, we are really talking about developing the power of meditative concentration. It is only through the power of meditative concentration that we can face the eight winds of gain, loss, defamation, honor, praise, ridicule, sorrow, and joy. Those who have the power of meditative concentration are unmoved by anger or joy and are not encumbered by happiness or suffering.

Those who successfully practice meditation can engage the wisdom within their intrinsic nature such that they are free from worry and fear even in the face of death. This is life at its happiest, and is a life that is free and liberated.

In Chinese, "meditative concentration" is made up of two characters: *chan* (禪) and *ding* (定). Though the two are very commonly found together, their meanings are slightly different. *Chan*, also known as *zen* in Japanese, refers to the practice of meditation. *Chan*, however, does not only refer to sitting meditation, but to all the moments in life which are infused with the flavor of a meditative mind. *Ding* refers to focusing the mind entirely upon a single point such that it has no more distractions and reaches a state of serene equanimity.

The *Treatise on the Perfection of Great Wisdom* says, "Meditative concentration is the settling of all distracting thoughts." Meditative concentration allows us to let go of our worries and purify the mind so that we can awaken to the Way. It is the method by which we can settle the mind into *samadhi*,[8] where it can abide in equanimity. Meditative concentration can energize the mind so that it is unmoved by external circumstances and is able to see intrinsic nature.

Meditation and the Chan School

Meditation has been a part of all Buddhist schools from the beginning. Even during the time of the Buddha, meditation was prevalent throughout India's religious landscape. When Buddhism came to China the founding masters of the Chan School, the Chinese meditation school, took the Indian emphasis on mental tranquility and brought it into everyday life. This created a kind of meditation that was both passive and active, which later developed

Gongans

A *gongan*, or *koan* in Japanese, is the story of an encounter between Chan practitioners that reveals some Chan wisdom. Many *gongans* record the short and somewhat playful exchanges between the great Chan masters of the past and their disciples, and are remembered and contemplated even today.

into the Chinese style of "practical meditation" and had a great influence on Chinese culture.

The oldest *gongan* of the Chan School is called "holding forth a flower, responding with a smile," and tells the story of the origin of the Chan School. One day, while the Buddha was at Vulture Peak, the Brahma king came to see him. The Brahma king gave the Buddha a golden flower and offered himself as a throne, imploring the Buddha to teach the Dharma so that all living beings would benefit. The Buddha then ascended atop the Brahma king and held up the golden flower so that the entire assembly could see it.

The assembly was composed of over one million human and celestial beings and they all looked at one another, unable to understand the meaning behind the Buddha's action. Only one of the Buddha's disciples, the venerable Mahakasyapa, understood what the Buddha meant, and smiled.

The Buddha then said, "I have the treasury of the true Dharma eye, the wondrous mind of *nirvana*, the true reality without form. It is a profound teaching that is not set down in written words, but is a separate transmission beyond the teachings. This I entrust to Mahakasyapa."

The Chan School traces its origin back to this initial transmission of the Dharma to Mahakasyapa at the Vulture Peak assembly. The teachings were transmitted from generation to generation until Bodhidharma, the twenty-eighth Chan Patriarch, came to China and became the first Chinese Patriarch. Bodhidharma was then succeeded in order by Huike, Sengcan, Daoxin, and Hongren.

Hongren, the Fifth Chan Patriarch, lived during the seventh century, and had two prominent disciples: Shenxiu and Huineng.

Shenxiu had been Hongren's leading disciple for many years. When asked to affirm his enlightenment by writing a poem, he composed the following verse:

> *The body is a bodhi tree,*
> *The mind is like a bright standing mirror;*
> *Diligently clean it at all times,*
> *So it does not attract dust.*

Huineng was a commoner from southern China who suddenly became enlightened when he heard one of Hongren's students reciting the *Diamond Sutra*. He then went to see Hongren and stayed at his temple. Having seen Shenxiu's poem, he wrote his own:

> *Essentially, bodhi is not a tree.*
> *The bright mirror is also not standing;*
> *Inherently, there is no thing,*
> *Where can it attract dust?*

Huineng's poem showed that he was enlightened and had seen his intrinsic nature. Later that night, Hongren transmitted the Dharma to Huineng in secret, naming him the Sixth Patriarch of the Chan School.

Huineng's teachings emphasized that we all intrinsically have Buddha nature, and that enlightenment can occur suddenly with a single thought. On the other hand, Shenxiu taught that enlightenment was possible only through gradual practice. Shenxiu would continue to be a prominent disciple during his lifetime, but it was from Huineng that the Chan School flourished in China, leading to the Five Houses and Seven Schools that we know today.

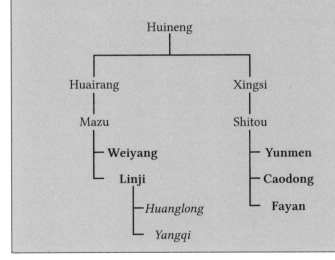

The Five Houses and the Seven Schools

All of the Chan Schools we know today are said to be directly connected to Huineng, the Sixth Patriarch of the Chan School. The "Five Houses of Chan" are descended from Huineng's two prominent disciples, Huairang and Xingsi. Two other schools, the Huanglong School and the Yangqi School descended from the Linji House. When the Five Houses and the two additional schools are counted together they are known as the "Seven Schools of Chan."

Huineng

Huairang — Mazu — Weiyang — Linji — Huanglong — Yangqi

Xingsi — Shitou — Yunmen — Caodong — Fayan

Though the teachings of the Chan School are known as a separate transmission beyond the teachings which cannot be set down in words, we should not disregard words entirely. Even Huineng said, "If people say 'the sutras do not function through words,' then there is no reason to have language. Language is itself formed with words. People also say that direct teachings are not established through words; but 'not' and 'established' are words!"

Chan does not suggest that we should not rely on the sutras at all. Instead it means that we should never become dogmatic about the sutras. Enlightenment is like the moon, and the sutras are like a finger pointing towards the moon. We must realize that the sutras and language itself are not enlightenment, but that they help lead us to understand the mind and see our intrinsic nature.

In order to liberate the world the Buddha and the ancient sages would enthusiastically give talks and compose texts, as well as praise and comment upon previous teachings. For this reason, countless volumes of Chan sayings and *gongans* have been compiled over the years. Though Chan may go by many different names and appear in different forms, they all share the same spirit and focus.

Chan is the core of the Buddhist teachings, the backbone of Chinese Buddhism, and the essence of Chinese culture. Master Taixu described it succinctly by saying, "The unique elements of Chinese Buddhism lie within Chan." Not only has Chan been a fundamental aspect of Chinese thought since the Tang and Song dynasties, but from the Song dynasty onward Chan became an important topic of inquiry for all philosophical traditions, including those of Confucius, Mencius, Laozi, and Zhuangzi.

Such Chan interpretations of Confucianism and the fusion of Chan and Confucian thought show the profound influence that Buddhism had upon Chinese history. As a result, any study of Buddhism must necessarily include Chan.

With the modern discovery of Chan texts at Dunhuang, China, academic circles have slowly started treating Chan studies more seriously. Internationally renowned scholars like Hu Shi, Lü Cheng, and D. T. Suzuki began devoting themselves to the study of Chan. The 20th century has seen an upsurge of interest in Chan

> ## Meditative Concentration and Wisdom in the Sutras
>
> The pairing of meditative concentration and wisdom is mentioned throughout the Buddhist sutras. For example, the northern version of the *Mahaparinirvana Sutra* states, "Only the equal cultivation of both meditative concentration and wisdom leads to formless *nirvana*."
>
> Another passage in the *Sutra on the Mahayana Practice of the Six Perfections* says, "Meditative concentration produces wisdom. Meditative concentration is also generated from wisdom. Meditative concentration and wisdom are the foundation of the Buddha's great enlightenment."

studies that began in mainland China and has swept across Europe and America.

The Role of Meditation

Any discussion of meditation will generally involve a discussion on sitting meditation. However, true meditation does do not lie in the formal practice of sitting meditation: it lies in developing energy in the mind. To practice meditation we must focus on stopping delusion and seeing truth, as well as equally developing both meditative concentration and wisdom.

Stopping delusion means using meditation to put an end to all deluded thoughts so that the mind is concentrated on a single point. Seeing truth means using meditation to open the mind to true wisdom, so that all phenomena can be seen correctly and all the bonds of affliction can be eliminated. "Stopping delusion" suggests a sort of passive defense and has more to do with meditative concentration, while "seeing truth" is a more active work of construction and is more closely aligned with the development of wisdom. The two are often considered inseparable: meditative concentration is the essence of wisdom, and wisdom is the function of meditative concentration. Both must be practiced so that meditative concentration and wisdom can come together, delusion can be eliminated, and truth realized.

Chan is the original nature of all living beings. That being said, meditative concentration cannot be attained just through sitting meditation. Sitting meditation alone does not necessarily lead to Buddhahood, just as polishing a tile will never make the tile into a mirror. However, meditative concentration *can* be cultivated through sitting meditation, and it still remains the introductory method for most beginners.

Chan is intimately connected with our normal, everyday lives. In this complex and confusing modern society, we must use the power of meditative concentration to stabilize our erratic minds and unsettled bodies.

Chapter Six

Enlightenment

The Goal of Meditative Concentration

To Seek Enlightenment

I T HAS BEEN said that the 21st century will be the Buddhist century, more specifically that it will be the century of meditation. Of course, meditation does not belong exclusively to Buddhism: meditation can be found in everyone's mind, and is a treasure that is shared by all of humanity.

When the Buddha held up the flower before the Vulture Peak assembly and transmitted the Chan teachings to Mahakasyapa, he also gave Chan to all living beings. Chan is like the energy of the sun, for as long as the sun hangs in the sky it shines down on the earth. In the same way, as long as we have our minds we can have the energy of Chan wherever we go. Chan is not supernatural, nor is it some mysterious phenomena. Chan is like the following verse:

> *The same old moon is seen out the window,*
> *When there are plum blossoms, it is no longer*
> *the same.*

The whole world is permeated by the subtleties of Chan, for there is nothing that appears in nature which is beyond its wondrous use.

Chan and meditation have spread from East to West, and has evolved from an exclusively monastic practice to a form of spiritual cultivation practiced by both monastics and laypeople. For modern people who live in this hectic society, sitting quietly for a few minutes each day and occasionally participating in meditation activities at a temple can give them the energy to continue on with their lives.

Sitting meditation is a skillful way to develop meditative concentration. Some people go astray because they practice sitting meditation to obtain supernatural powers or experience occult phenomena. Others practice sitting meditation to become Buddhas, but such a commitment is insufficient and follows the wrong method. Thus, nothing comes from all of their efforts.

Generations of Chan masters practiced Chan not to become Buddhas, but to seek enlightenment. One cannot become a Buddha by searching for it. Rather, it takes a long period of practice to become a Buddha, requiring three great *kalpas*[9] to perfect one's wisdom and merit, and one hundred small *kalpas* to perfect the supreme marks.[10] Rather than seeking to become a Buddha, one should strive to perfect one's wisdom and merit. Once these qualities have been perfected, one will naturally become a Buddha.

The most important thing to remember about sitting meditation is that all of the work done to develop meditative concentration must carry over to your everyday life. The Buddha's teachings must be experienced in your daily activities before there can be any meditation. Meditation cannot be divorced from daily life. You cannot see deeply into the mind apart from work and service.

The daily life of a Chan practitioner cannot be separated from their work, just as fish cannot live without water and trees cannot grow without soil. A Chan practitioner's daily labors are the provisions which support him on the path. Many Chan masters became enlightened while bent over piles of split wood or shouldering heavy loads as part of their daily work. The Chan Master Xiangyan Zhixian became enlightened while hoeing and tilling a field. Dongshan Liangjie became enlightened when he caught a glimpse of his own shadow in a river. In Japan, the National Master Muso became enlightened as he slept leaning against a wall. The monk Xuyun became enlightened upon breaking a teacup. Yongming Yanshou became enlightened when he heard the sound of some firewood hitting the ground, and there are many other similar cases.

Enlightenment is the true goal of developing meditative concentration. For an enlightened Chan master mountains are still mountains and rivers are still rivers – the difference is that the mountains, rivers, and the great earth itself become one with the Chan master, and can be used as he pleases. The Way is within you; it is not something that can be sought outside of you. Therefore, to become enlightened you can only rely on yourself, for enlightenment can only be realized on your own.

A novice monk once asked Chan Master Zhaozhou Congshen, "How should one learn the Way? How should meditation be practiced? How does one become enlightened? How does one attain Buddhahood?"

Chan Master Zhaozhou nodded his head, stood up, and said, "I don't have time to speak with you, I have to take a piss."

The Chan master started to walk away, ignoring the novice's astonishment. After a few steps, he suddenly stopped, looked back,

What is the Way?

The Chinese character *dao* (道), "the Way," has long been a part of Chinese philosophy. In Buddhism, the Way refers both to the way we should live, as well as the way things are. The Way is the truth of Buddhism, as it exists in the world around us and within ourselves.

and said with a smile, "You asked me such big questions – but even something as simple as peeing I still must do myself. How can you do it for me?"

The Path to Enlightenment

One can seek enlightenment by practicing meditation, but how should we practice so that we can attain enlightenment? Total and complete enlightenment is not attained easily. One must develop small moments of insight and understanding each day. These small, daily bits of enlightenment accumulate over time, until they culminate in a sudden flash of great enlightenment.

Enlightenment requires the right causes and conditions to occur, for only when things fall perfectly into place can one develop understanding. It is much like how a radio must be tuned to the right frequency to produce sound, or a camera must be focused correctly to capture a sharp image.

Chan Master Mazu Daoyi was a prominent monastic who lived during the Tang dynasty. After his enlightenment he returned to his home village, where his sister-in-law treated him with extraordinary respect. She honored him as a teacher, and asked him how she could become enlightened. Mazu Daoyi answered her, "Take a chicken egg and hang it in midair, then listen to it carefully every day. When you hear the egg make a sound, then you will be enlightened; that's all it takes!"

His sister-in-law believed him, suspended a chicken egg as he instructed, and listened to it every day to see if she could hear any sound. Many years passed and she did not hear a sound, but she never neglected her practice. Over time, the string from which the egg hung slowly began to rot until one day it broke. The egg dropped through the air and hit the ground with a *crack*. When Mazu Daoyi's sister-in-law heard this, she became enlightened.

The self and exterior things are originally one, for there has never been a real world outside of the mind. The sound of the egg cracking broke through the distinction between internal and external, and the separation between the self and others. As long as one's thoughts are unified and one's spirit is concentrated even insentient objects can teach the path to enlightenment.

There have been many great monks and sages who attained enlightenment, though their methods of doing so are sometimes quite strange. Some have become enlightened suddenly upon seeing flowers bloom or fall. Others became enlightened upon hearing a bubbling spring or the sound of frogs croaking. Some became enlightened upon breaking a cup or a plate.

Enlightenment must be directly experienced and is not something an average person can wildly speculate about. Those who casually imitate the words and actions of Chan practitioners without doing the work to attain enlightenment will fall short and invite the ridicule of those who truly know.

Once a young man was sitting in meditation when an old Chan master passed by. Though the young man noticed the Chan master, he did not rise to greet him. The Chan master then scolded him, "How can a young person like you not stand and greet an older person? Have you no common courtesy?"

The young man tried to imitate the style of a wise Chan practitioner and said, "To greet you sitting down is to greet you standing up!"

The old Chan master heard this, stepped forward, and slapped the young man on the face.

"Why did you hit me?" the young man responded angrily.

The Chan master responded with a smile, "To slap you is to not slap you."

Chan is not about seeing who is smarter using ordinary knowledge, nor is it something that can be imitated by putting on an act. The wisdom of enlightenment radiates forth naturally and is not something that can be attained by guesswork or copying others.

The Wisdom of Enlightenment

The wisdom of enlightenment is different from other kinds of knowledge. Knowledge may come from direct experience, like when someone hits me and I think, "Ouch, that hurts!" or when my stomach is growling and I think, "Boy, am I hungry." Knowledge can be feeling happy or sad, distinguishing what is good and bad, and understanding what is right and wrong. All of these are kinds of knowledge, but they are not the same as the wisdom of enlightenment.

When Sir Isaac Newton saw an apple fall to the ground, he developed knowledge of gravity. Benjamin Franklin's knowledge of electricity set in motion the development of electrical science, resulting in so much of the technology we have today. These discoveries are not the same as enlightenment, though the accumulation of knowledge has led us to develop scientific understanding which has greatly benefited humanity.

When the Buddha sat under the bodhi tree he attained perfect and complete enlightenment, and as he watched the twinkling stars that night he said, "Marvelous, marvelous! All sentient beings have the Tathagata's wisdom and virtue, but they fail to realize it because they cling to deluded thoughts and attachments." This is the wisdom of enlightenment that comes from spiritual practice.

Enlightenment is finding something that was hidden. It is a sudden flash of light that makes us exclaim, "Ah, I have found it!" It is searching for the source of life, and finding your original face. It is like being transported back to your hometown and seeing the faces of your parents after many years of absence.

Enlightenment can make you laugh for three days. All the rivers and mountains on earth appear like family, and every mountain peak for thousands of miles seems like an old friend. Enlightenment can also make you cry for three days, like a weary son who returns to the embrace of his loving mother after a long absence, shedding tears of gratitude when there is nothing more to be said. Enlightenment is an unequivocal conception. Enlightenment is the power of penetrating insight. Enlightenment is awakening to your own intrinsic nature. Enlightenment is complete understanding.

Enlightenment is the realization that many things which seem very different are actually one. An enlightened person sees life and death as one, and knows that life is not always joyful and death is not always sad. An enlightened person sees motion and stillness as one, for within this world of constant change and motion there is the tranquility of *nirvana*, and within that tranquility there are countless beings who live a thriving and active life. An enlightened person sees existence and non-existence as one, for as wonderful as existence is, it is only from non-existence that the millions of forms of existence can arise. An enlightened person sees coming and going as one, for what has come has not truly come, what has gone is not truly gone, and the gathering of family and the departing of old friends is one and the same.

Enlightenment allows us to see unity where there seem to be contradictions, and discover simplicity from within complexity. It allows us to find an open path amidst many obstacles, and liberation from the chains that bind us.

Enlightenment involves both revelation and unawareness. Enlightenment is like a sudden flash of light within the darkness that shines through the cloud of ignorance and reveals the brightness of the world. This is the revelation that comes from enlightenment. On the other hand, after all has been revealed, one looks back on the world and on the delusion of the past and realizes just how unaware one was. This is the unawareness that comes from enlightenment.

The unenlightened mind has many attachments. When people are not yet enlightened they hunger for fame and fortune, are bothered by conflict and disagreements with others, and wallow in the illusion of love and romance. They cannot let go of these things and are unable to liberate themselves. After enlightenment, you can break free from the bonds of fame and fortune and break through the confusion of love's desire. With an enlightened mind you are able to view the world with clarity and assume your proper place in the universe.

Enlightenment encompasses everything from your ideas to how you live your life. An enlightened life is a life of freedom where one is open to all conditions as they arise. It is a life which is natural, true, and beautiful, and is beyond all comparisons.

Someone once asked Chan Master Zhaozhou Congshen, "Why did Bodhidharma come from the West?"

The Chan master responded, "Go drink tea!"

This person asked a second question, "What was my original face before I was born?"

The Chan master responded, "Go wash your alms bowl!"

What is the relationship between drinking tea, washing the alms bowl, and attaining enlightenment? They are more closely related than you may think. If we can taste the subtle flavor of wisdom in the food we eat and the tea we drink, then we will be able to see our original face and know the teachings of all the Buddhas of the past, present, and future. The Buddhist teachings are not to be sought in lofty places. Instead we should experience them with an ordinary mind that is natural and simple.

After enlightenment, wisdom becomes more important than feelings and one's own biases become purified. One is able to experience the eternity of time and the infinity of space.

Once, Chan Master Zhitong suddenly arose from his bed in the middle of the night and yelled out, "I'm enlightened, I'm enlightened!"

The entire monastic community at the temple was awakened by the racket he made. Chan Master Guizong Zhichang asked him in all seriousness, "What have you become enlightened about?"

Zhitong replied without a moment's hesitation: "That all female practitioners are originally women!" Such an answer is really something. That female practitioners are women is such an ordinary fact, but to truly understand it is to be enlightened to the fact that all phenomena are universally equal. That is true enlightenment.

Enlightenment happens naturally and at just the right moment. It is not something that can be expressed or described in words. It is similar to someone eating some candy. Even if he tried to explain the candy's sweetness until he lost his voice all his explanations would be meaningless, for only he is able to know exactly what the candy tastes like. The sweetness of the candy can only be experienced by eating it. In the same way, you can only experience enlightenment for yourself. This is why the Chan School says that enlightenment cannot be spoken in words and is beyond language.

Though enlightenment cannot be easily communicated in language, it can absolutely be experienced. Enlightenment can reveal the profound mysteries of life, and show that life contains unlimited happiness. Enlightenment shows us that time is endless, and that a single instant can encompass all of eternity. Enlightenment lets us understand that space is boundless; that each flower can contain a world and each leaf can contain a Buddha. Enlightenment lets us realize that other people and ourselves are one, and that living beings and Buddhas are the same.

The sound of enlightenment is the *crack* of ignorance being broken, and it can occur ten thousand times faster than a flash of lightning. It is the shattering of empty space, the annihilation of delusion, and a bright light before our eyes.

The Moment of Enlightenment

Enlightenment is an extraordinarily rapid, sudden, and unexpected state. However, enlightenment is not something that is accomplished in a single stroke. Enlightenment too has its stages. The great Song dynasty poet Su Shi had great insights about meditation and composed three poems describing the stages of enlightenment. The first stage is the situation before developing meditative concentration:

It's a mountain range when viewed horizontally, a
*   peak vertically;*
Near, far, high, or low—how its appearance varies.
One cannot know the true nature of Mt. Lu;
For one is on that very mountain itself.

The second poem describes the state where one is in meditation but has not yet attained enlightenment:

Misty rain over Mt. Lu and the waves of Zhejiang,
Missing out on such marvels brings a thousand
*   unbearable regrets;*
But upon actually seeing them, there is nothing
*   really there:*
Just misty rain over Mt. Lu and the waves of
*   Zhejiang.*

The third poem describes the state after attaining enlightenment:

The sounds of the rippling creek are all words of
*   the Buddha;*
The mountain scene is none other than the body of
*   the Dharma.*
Night falls, and one contemplates eighty-four
*   thousand verses,*
Just how will I tell others these truths at some
*   later time?*

Before attaining enlightenment one sees the world through clouded vision, unable to understand the true nature of things. After attaining enlightenment, one looks upon all the world's phenomena like a blind person who can now see. One can now see with true clarity the original nature of the mountains, rivers, and the great earth itself.

Before one is enlightened, one is unwilling to eat when it's time to eat and ponders a hundred thoughts, and one is unwilling to sleep when it's time to sleep and considers a thousand plans. After one is enlightened, one eats when hungry and sleeps when tired. Those who are enlightened still eat and sleep, but now they have the freedom to do as they please and go wherever they wish. Before attaining enlightenment, each moment is hard to bear, and each step is a difficult burden; but after attaining enlightenment, every day is a good day, and everywhere is a smooth and open road.

After Enlightenment

What happens after enlightenment? You get back to your practice! Even if you attain enlightenment, if you do not practice, you will never become a Buddha. While some practice first and become enlightened later, others become enlightened first and practice later. Whichever comes first, enlightenment or spiritual practice, upon enlightenment one must continue to cultivate according to the path and practice according to the teachings. One must practice in this human world by serving others and nourishing the conditions for merit and wisdom. When all the causes and conditions are in place, one will naturally attain enlightenment and become a Buddha. This is why all Buddhas become enlightened in the human world.

Chan practitioners are humanistic because they have developed meditative concentration for generations and seek enlightenment rather than attaining Buddhahood. After attaining enlightenment in this human world, they are liberated in the present moment of their lives. They find peace and freedom in body and mind, understand the mind, and see their nature. All of this comes from enlightenment—why worry about being unable to become a Buddha?

Meditative concentration is a part of life; it's not just sitting meditation. Sitting meditation is a way to train the mind to develop concentration, and is a skillful method for generating the power of meditative concentration. Chan practitioners must never indulge in the bliss of sitting meditation, lest they forget Buddhism's mission in the world and forget that learning meditation means breathing out of the same nostrils as all living beings. Developing meditative concentration puts you in sync with the pulse of the whole universe. This should be the intention of all Chan practitioners in the world.

Chapter Seven

Meditation Explained

The Practice of Meditative Concentration

What is Meditation?

ONE OF THE great advantages of sitting meditation is that you can take it with you wherever you go. Whether you are in a forest deep in the mountains or beside a stream among the grass and reeds, you can develop meditative concentration just by sitting down and crossing your legs.

But what is meditation? Does it come from sitting, standing, or lying down? Huineng, the Sixth Patriarch of the Chan School, said that meditative concentration is not found in any of these positions. In fact, Huineng once told Chan Master Zhicheng, "Abiding with the mind contemplating stillness is sickness, not Chan."

How should we practice meditation? The great Chan Master Zibo once said:

> *Without delving into the mind, sitting meditation is*
> *a pointless exercise for increasing suffering;*

If you can guard your thoughts, even blaming the
Buddha can be beneficial to your practice.

Meditation is not about sitting quietly with your eyes closed—
this is just one method for developing meditative concentration.
What matters in meditation is being able to contemplate and focus
the mind. Chan Master Nanyue Huairang once said, "Consider an
ox pulling a cart: if the cart does not move, do you hit the cart or do
you hit the ox?" Beating the cart is useless. In the same way, how
you concentrate the mind is far more important than what you do
with the body.

Chan Master Ruiyan, who lived during the Tang dynasty,
would often say to himself, "Master, are you there? Yes; yes, I am!"
Most people will think someone like this is crazy, but those who
know about meditation can appreciate his profound words. Chan
Master Ruiyan was trying to awaken to his intrinsic nature, and
thus never left the present moment even for an instant.

To practice meditation, one must focus on the present
moment, stop delusion, and see the mind. In China, the Chan
School encouraged the development of meditative concentration
through communal labor, like carrying firewood and water. This
training allowed Chan practitioners to see their intrinsic nature
by illuminating their minds, thus achieving the ultimate goal of
meditative concentration.

The Fundamentals of Sitting Meditation

While it is true that meditative concentration is not *about* sitting,
sitting meditation is still a necessary practice for beginners. Sitting
meditation is required to experience the joys of meditation and
to begin to contemplate and investigate one's intrinsic nature.

Proper Meditation Posture

It is very important to have correct posture when practicing sitting meditation. The proper posture for sitting meditation is made up of seven points:

1. Sit straight with your legs crossed, putting the right foot on the left thigh and the left foot on the right thigh.
2. Form the hands into the mudra and place them in your lap.
3. Keep the back straight and do not lean against a wall.
4. Keep the head and neck straight.
5. Relax your shoulders so they are balanced and natural, and the chest is flat.
6. Lightly join the lips together and place the top of the tongue on the upper palate.
7. Close your eyes halfway, look downward and contemplate the mind.

To begin the practice of sitting meditation, it is important to have some basic meditation knowledge and be familiar with the fundamentals.

Meditation has been explained in many different ways in many different texts throughout the centuries, and while no explanation can give a complete picture of what meditation is, they all contain valuable teachings. For example, the sixth century text, the *Condensed Techniques for Stopping Delusion and Seeing Truth* describes the beginnings of sitting meditation as having balanced meals, balanced rest, a balanced body, balanced breathing, and a balanced mind.

The Six Sublime Methods

Another such teaching is the "Six Sublime Methods." The Six Sublime Methods were formulated by Zhiyi, the founder to the Tiantai School, and are six methods of meditation practice that lead to *nirvana*. The Six Sublime Methods are:

1. Counting the breath

This first sublime method is to focus the mind by counting the breaths (from one to ten). It is an essential practice for developing meditative concentration.

2. Following the breath

In the second sublime method, one follows the breath during inhales and exhales without counting the breaths. This is an easy and natural way to develop meditative concentration.

3. Stopping Delusion

The third sublime method is to make the mind still and tranquil by putting an end to the mind's delusions and abiding in a state of non-thought. Once one has put a stop to these delusions the mind will naturally become concentrated and wisdom will arise.

4. Seeing Truth

Often paired with the previous method, the fourth sublime method is to see deeply into all phenomena and develop wisdom. This is often done by contemplating the five aggregates. The five aggregates are the five different things that make up a living being: form, feeling, perception, mental formations, and consciousness. When practicing this method each of the five aggregates are seen to be false. In this way, one can break through delusion and develop skillful, undefiled wisdom.

5. Self-reflection

When reflecting on the mind, one knows that the idea that the mind is the "knower" is untrue, and thus the attachment to the self will disappear on its own. Then the skillful wisdom without outflows will make all things clear.

6. Purification

When the mind is free of attachments, everything becomes clear and pure. One develops wisdom that is truly clear and without outflows. This naturally brings an end to confusion and allows one to realize the truth.

Of all of the six sublime methods, following the breath is the most important, for one sees the breath move from activity to tranquility. After contemplating the breath, one can also see the mind move from activity to tranquility. The breath moves in and out, just like the cycle of birth and death, or the arising and ceasing of phenomena. It is by seeing the breath that we can come to realize the Buddhist teaching that all things are impermanent, suffering, and empty. Once this is understood the attachment to the self is severed, and the higher states of self-reflection and purification are possible.

The Five Contemplations

Another meditation teaching is the "Five Contemplations." Before we achieve meditative concentration, we can use the

five contemplations to eliminate specific afflictions. The Five
Contemplations are:

1. The Contemplation of Impurity

To practice the contemplation of impurity visualize all the
filth and muck contained within your body and the bodies of
others. This contemplation is used to counteract desire.

2. The Contemplation of Compassion

This contemplation is for people who are prone to anger, and
involves visualizing how true happiness can be obtained by
removing suffering and offering happiness. By visualizing

The Twelve Links of Dependent Origination

The Twelve Links of Dependent Origination is the Buddhist
analysis of the causes and conditions which lead to life. Each
link in the chain is the cause that gives rise to the next link, and
each link can be broken by removing the link preceding it. The
twelve links are:

1. Ignorance
2. Mental formations
3. Consciousness
4. Name and form
5. The six sense organs
6. Contact
7. Feeling
8. Craving
9. Clinging
10. Becoming
11. Birth
12. Aging and death

in this way, practitioners are able to diffuse their anger and hatred.

3.   The Contemplation of Causes and Conditions

People remain ignorant and develop attachments because they fail to realize that all phenomena in the world arise and cease because of causes and conditions. By investigating and understanding causes and conditions ignorance transforms into wisdom. When contemplating causes and conditions, one sees all Twelve Links of Dependent Origination in every thought and understands that each thought arises from a previous thought in an endless series of preceding and succeeding thoughts. All things in life arise due to causes, and all things will produce effects. By understanding this, one can see how each individual is connected to all of humanity, and how any isolated event is connected to every other.

4.   The Contemplation of Counting the Breath

When the mind is swirling with deluded thoughts we can contemplate the breath as a way to focus the mind. Not only will this make our breathing even, but it frees the mind of distractions and allows us to attain a state of inner calm.

5.   The Contemplation of the Buddha

In this form of contemplation we are mindful of the Buddha's radiant features, his accomplishments, and his tranquility, as a way to overcome our karmic obstacles.

The Four Bases of Mindfulness

Another meditation teaching is the "Four Bases of Mindfulness." The Four Bases of Mindfulness allow us to use our mindfulness so that we do not mistake impurity for purity, suffering for happiness, impermanence for permanence, and what has no independent self for something that does. They are:

1. Mindfulness of the Body

One is mindful of the body, and contemplates the impure aspects of the body. At the same time, one contemplates the compounded nature of the body, its impermanence, suffering, emptiness, and lack of selfhood. In this way, one counteracts the delusion of seeing the impure as pure.

2. Mindfulness of Feelings

One is mindful of feelings and observes how pursuing happiness can have the opposite effect of producing the causes for suffering. One also contemplates feelings' characteristics of suffering and emptiness. In this way, one counteracts the delusion of seeing suffering as happiness.

3. Mindfulness of the Mind

One is mindful of the mind and contemplates the impermanence of the mind as the "seeker" by contemplating the arising and ceasing of thoughts. In this way, one counteracts the delusion of seeing impermanence as permanence.

4. Mindfulness of Phenomena

One is mindful of phenomena, and contemplates how all phenomena arise due to causes and conditions and have no self-nature. In this way, one counteracts the delusion of seeing what has no self as having a self.

Though sitting meditation was given to us from the ancient past it is a way for modern people to lead happy lives. Sitting meditation allows us to dispel the pressures of daily life that come from the mind's confusion and a mistaken understanding of phenomena. Practicing sitting meditation quiets the mind and stills our thoughts so that we can recover our intrinsic nature.

Sitting meditation makes us healthier. The sutras say, "When the mind arises, all phenomena arise." Modern medical science has proven that much of our sickness comes from our emotions, such as worry, greed, and anger. Meditation can give us a peaceful temperament, allows us to breathe calmly, and makes us feel refreshed. Sitting meditation also enhances circulation and boosts metabolism, thereby staving off the degeneration of bodily functions.

Sitting meditation enhances our morality. In today's society with its technological advances and material abundance, most people spend their days restlessly seeking after material pleasures, fame, position, and power, such that they cloud their minds with desire and lose sense of who they are. But, if these people can befriend sitting meditation they will become their own masters and will no longer be slaves to material things. They will be able to elevate their morality and transform their disposition.

Sitting meditation allows us to enjoy the bliss of meditative concentration. The Buddha once said, "One who sits in meditation gains Dharma joy." The Dharma joy mentioned by the Buddha is the bliss of meditative concentration. This bliss is created by a tranquil mind and cannot be compared to the happiness of the five desires. Those who diligently practice sitting meditation can obtain this bliss.

Sitting meditation develops our wisdom. The *Suramgama Sutra* says, "Take focusing the mind as your precepts. Meditative concentration arises from the precepts; wisdom arises from meditative concentration." Sitting meditation calms the body and spirit and purifies the mind. This not only makes us wiser, but it will win us everyone's love and respect and make things easier to accomplish. Sitting meditation is the path to cultivating merit and wisdom.

The practice of sitting meditation allows us to become Buddhas by seeing our intrinsic nature. Sitting meditation eliminates affliction and deluded thoughts, allowing us to be quiet both within and without. When the mind reaches *nirvana*, it expands into enlightenment. This is why a meditation hall is also called the Buddha's court. As long as we put in the effort, we will be able to see our nature and become Buddhas.

The final goal of sitting meditation is to free the body and mind. We must free ourselves from all forms of delusion and all discriminating thoughts, such that even the world of the Buddha and enlightenment is washed away without a trace. Amid the silence of ancient temples, Chan masters sat in meditation, burning stick after stick of incense. They dedicated their lives to the practice of sitting meditation, with their goal being to put an end to this world of delusion. They hoped that by constantly meditating they could purify their original mind and merge into time and space, reaching a liberated state of total freedom beyond enlightenment or delusion.

The Roadmap to Meditative Concentration

The meditative experience is difficult to describe, and for this reason it can sometimes be difficult to know where you are along the path. Thankfully, the great Chan masters of the past have devised ways for us to know what the state of our cultivation is, and how much further we have to go.

The Nine Stages of Mental Focus

One of these methods is called the "Nine Stages of Mental Focus." Once you have been meditating for a while, these nine stages can be used to measure the progress of your practice. The Nine Stages of Mental Focus are:

1. Internal Focus

When practicing meditation the very first step is to concentrate the mind on a single point, so that the mind's focus turns inward and is free from external distractions.

2. Continuous Focus

When the coarse mind is first applied to a meditation object, it cannot yet focus universally and impartially. When the mind discerns external phenomena, continually apply the mind to the object of meditation, clarifying and purifying it, until the mind becomes refined.

3. Calm Focus

Even if the mind can maintain its internal focus and continuous focus, there will still be moments of lost and distracted thought. Notice as soon as the mind wanders off, and bring its focus back to the meditation object.

4.   Close Focus

At this point false thoughts and distractions no longer arise in the mind. The mind is able to detect false thoughts before they arise and subdue them. The mind no longer focuses on anything external, thus it is called "close focus."

5.   Compliance

In this state one understands the wondrous virtues of meditation and the nature of the ten distractions: those that arise from forms, sounds, smells, taste, touch, greed, anger, ignorance, men, and women. With this knowledge, one is able to control the mind and prevent movement and distraction.

6.   Quiescence

In this state one's false seeking, thinking, and the minor afflictions are subdued by one's virtue of calmness, and the mind is tamed so that it is free of distractions.

7.   Supreme Quiescence

In this state, when false thinking, seeking, and the minor afflictions arise they are immediately cast out.

8.   One-Pointed Focus

In this state, through effort and practice, the power of meditative concentration becomes continuous.

9.   Equilibrium

In this state, one's practice is now perfected from previous cultivation. One can maintain focus continuously and freely without any effort.

The Eight Dhyana States

Another way to understand meditation is by understanding the "Eight Dhyana States." *Dhyana* is a Sanskrit word which means "absorption," and describes a state in which the mind has become so focused and so concentrated that it attains a state of purity. Each of the dhyana states follows the previous one, and is a state of even more refined purity.

The Eight Dhyana States also serve as a guide to Buddhist cosmology. In Buddhism there is not only one realm of existence, but three: the desire realm, the form realm, and the formless realm. The desire realm encompasses the human and animal realm, as well as the six desire heavens and the hells. Beings that live in the desire realm are filled with desire. The first four dhyana states correspond to the form realm, where beings have no desire for food or sex and live with greater refinement and purity. The first four dhyana states are:

The First Dhyana

In this state, the mind is pure and no defilements are present. All affliction and desire have been eliminated, and the mind is without worries or desires.

The Second Dhyana

In this state, one no longer seeks out and analyzes phenomena. One's faith becomes pure and bright and free of seeking, analyzing, realizing, or contemplating, and one naturally attains happiness.

The Third Dhyana

In this state the happiness of the second dhyana is abandoned so that all that remains is a quiet and profound joy in which the mind is calm and at ease. This state is also known as the state of "profound joy that abandons happiness."

The Fourth Dhyana
In this state even the quiet and profound joy of the third dhyana is abandoned and all that remains are the activities of the consciousness, which are indifferent to all feelings.

The last four dhyana states are also called the "formless states," because they correspond to the formless realm. They are:

The Dhyana of Limitless Space
This state goes beyond the fourth dhyana and removes all form seen by the eye consciousness, as well as all feelings from the ears, nose, tongue, and body. All unwholesome thoughts and all thoughts that hinder concentration are abandoned, leaving the mind's consciousness concentrated on limitless space.

The Dhyana of Limitless Consciousness
In the previous dhyana, the conscious mind pervades all space. Since space is limitless, the mind will begin to become unfocused again. Thus one turns away from space and focuses the mind on consciousness. Thus the mind's concentration becomes unshakable. In this state, all consciousness of the past, present, and future appear such that the mind is free from distraction. This state is calm, secure, pure, and tranquil.

The Dhyana of Nothingness
By abandoning the state of limitless consciousness, one diligently focuses on nothingness. The mind becomes pure and attains tranquility with ease. In this state no thoughts arise.

The Dhyana of neither Thought nor Non-Thought
The state of limitless consciousness involves thought, while the state of nothingness involves non-thought. In this state, both previous states are abandoned such that neither thought nor non-thought remains. Neither existence nor non-existence manifest, and one is able to remain in the tranquility of cessation. No form of meditative concentration throughout the three realms can surpass it, and thus it is known as the "Divine Dhyana of neither Thought nor Non-Thought."

The Eight Dhyana States are the foundation of meditative concentration. When the Buddha became enlightened and when he entered *parinirvana* he relied upon these Eight Dhyana States for support. Their importance cannot possibly be overlooked.

The Humanistic Buddhist Practice of Meditation

The word "meditation" may create the image of an old monk who sits with his eyes cast downward in deep concentration, but this is not all there is to meditation. Huineng, the Sixth Patriarch of the Chan School, once said, "The Way is awakened to from the mind. How can it be from sitting?" Huineng also wrote a poem about the futility of relying on the body's sitting to develop meditative concentration:

> *In life, it sits without lying down*
> *In death, it lies down and does not sit,*
> *A pile of smelly bones.*
> *Why work so hard for it?*

Meditation is not about debating the merits of sitting or lying down. Once you have developed meditative concentration it does not matter if you are walking, standing, sitting, lying down, carrying firewood, or bringing water—every single action can suddenly lead to enlightenment and seeing intrinsic nature. Chan Master Yongjia Xuanjue once said, "Walking is meditation and sitting is meditation. With speech or silence, motion or stillness, the body remains peaceful and calm." For true Chan practitioners meditation is whatever they see in their daily lives; it is everywhere.

Humanistic Buddhism strives to bring meditation into daily life. It advocates using our ordinary, everyday mind, for there is no greater understanding. It challenges us to be constant in our faith, but to use our loving kindness, compassion, joy, and equanimity to adapt to the changing world. It asks us to practice diligently but simply, in a way in which we cherish our blessings, abide by the precepts, and live contentedly. It tells us to see the Buddha within our own minds, and to carry out all our daily tasks with confidence and perseverance. It requires that we apply ourselves in a dynamic, animated and lively way. Humanistic Buddhism lets us see that the Way is everywhere, and that there are infinite possibilities.

Youyuan once asked Chan Master Dazhu Huihai, "How can I personally practice well?"

Chan master Dazhu answered him, "Eat when you are hungry and sleep when you are tired."

Youyuan did not understand the Chan master and asked, "Does this mean every person is practicing every day?"

Chan Master Dazhu replied, "It's not the same. When people eat they pick the fat or the lean and are unwilling to eat their fill. When people sleep they have all sorts of wild fantasies and scheme in ten thousand ways."

Chan has always been humanistic, and all Chan masters since ancient times have developed meditative concentration and attained enlightenment from their daily labors. It was only through the passage of time that Chan slowly lost its original character and became like a piece of dry wood. Humanistic Buddhism is a fresh reintroduction of meditation's place in daily life. I hope that meditation in daily life can be the key that opens up the confused minds of human beings.

Putting on clothes and eating can be meditation. Walking and sleeping can be meditation. Even going to the bathroom can be meditation! The *Diamond Sutra* describes the Buddha's wisdom in his daily conduct: how he dressed, how he carried his alms bowl, and how he gathered alms. He wore clothes and ate like everyone else, but did so with enlightenment.

The Buddha's teachings are not disconnected from the secular world, and it is not necessary to isolate oneself deep in the mountains to practice meditation. There is no gap between meditation and the world. When one is able to cool the fires of anger and hatred, then everywhere becomes like a cool mountain stream. When the mind is at peace even a bustling crowd can be like a temple.

In my own life as a monk I have spent many years practicing meditation, and though I may not have gained much, I have had the opportunity to contact the deeper meaning of Chan on a few occasions.

In the 1950s Taiwan was still under martial law and people were not allowed to gather freely. I went to many different villages to teach Buddhism, and each time a police officer would come and try to break us up. Once I was giving a lecture when another police officer came to interfere.

He shouted an order at me: "Tell these people to disperse!"

I answered him plainly, "Wait until I finish speaking and they will disperse on their own."

In the year 2000, Nan Tien Temple, a Fo Guang Shan branch in Australia, was completed and I was asked to conduct the consecration ceremony for the Buddha statue. Ross Cameron, a member of the Australian House of Representatives, had been invited to the event as well, and he asked me, "Of all the world's religious leaders, who is the best?"

To this I told him, "The one you like is the best."

On another occasion, I was once asked if my teachings were aligned with capitalism or communism. I responded by saying, "They are not capitalism or communism, they are Buddha-ism!"

Chan is not to be discussed and researched, for its purpose is to improve our lives. Chan brings us all the wealth of the universe. Chan allows us to live; it is the food we drink and the clothes we wear. In the world of a Chan practitioner, some tattered cloth is enough to keep him warm and simple vegetables are enough to cure his hunger. Chan practitioners are one with nature, and wander freely and easily as conditions arise. In a single word, Chan is natural.

In the Chan School, an individual's practice and level of realization are very important. Nothing will come of speaking theoretically or echoing what others have said. Only by experiencing things directly can one understand the essence of Chan and preserve the true meaning of Buddhism.

You can lead a horse to water, but if he will not open his mouth he will die of thirst. In the same way the Buddhist sutras are a compass that can guide us to the truth, but we must walk the path ourselves. Once we understand something we must put it into practice. Only then will we be able to drink from the sweet water of the Dharma.

Chapter Eight

The Good Life

The Effects of Meditative Concentration

Living in the World and Living in the Mind

WE ALL LIVE in this world, and because we live in the world we cannot separate ourselves from society and our families, nor can we ignore the material world of money and wealth. In the outside world we constantly face the five desires of wealth, sex, food and drink, fame, and sleep and are confronted with the things that we see, hear, smell, taste, touch, and think about. However, what gives us the most pressure and is hardest to deal with is what is inside: our defiled thoughts of greed, anger, and ignorance. This is why we meditate and practice Buddhism: to give ourselves mental defenses and spiritual armor to strengthen the power of the mind.

How can we counter the five desires, the six sense objects and our greed, anger, and ignorance? The *Diamond Sutra* says, "The mind should not abide in sight, sound, smell, taste, touch, or dharmas."[11] This means that the mind should not become fixated on any of the six sense objects—it should not become attached to external "form." This is because, as is said elsewhere in the sutra, any notion of a self, a person, a sentient being, or a lifespan is unreal; and each of the six senses is contaminated. When we have greed, attachment, and anxiety towards our mental states and hold to the notion of a self we will develop wrong views, and these wrong views naturally give rise to defiled and deluded thoughts.

The *Diamond Sutra* also says "Let the mind be present without an abode," for the mind must be able to abide nowhere before it can resist the five desires and the six sense objects. This is the only way that we can find freedom in every thought.

Once, Chan Master Daoshu and his disciples built a monastery that just so happened to have a Daoist temple as a neighbor. The Daoists did not look kindly on having the Buddhists next to them, and used magic spells to harass and terrorize the Buddhist practitioners. Some of the younger novices were frightened away, but Chan Master Daoshu continued to reside there for the next dozen years or so. In the end, the Daoists exhausted all their

 The Sixth Sense of Buddhism

One of the ways that Buddhism tries to understand the world is by understanding how we come to know it: through our senses. Each of our sense organs produces a different kind of consciousness when it interacts with the appropriate sense object. For example, the eyes see forms and produce sight, while the ears hear sounds and produce hearing. However, in Buddhism we also have a sixth sense: the mind. The mind, after all, is a sense organ not unlike our eyes, ears, nose, tongue, and body. The sense objects of the mind are called *dharmas* – these are the things that our mind thinks about to produce mental consciousness.

mystical powers. They finally realized that all they could do was move their temple someplace else. Someone asked Chan Master Daoshu, "Master, the Daoists have extensive supernatural abilities and their mystical powers are limitless. How were you able to defeat them?"

Daoshu replied, "I had no ability that could defeat them. The only thing I had was 'nothing.'"

"How could you defeat them with 'nothing?'"

Daoshu explained, "The Daoists had 'something:' they had their magic spells and supernatural powers. But 'something' has limits and boundaries. It is finite and can be exhausted. On the other hand, I had 'nothing,' which has no limits or boundaries. It is infinite and inexhaustible. The relationship between nothing and something is the same as the relationship between the unchanging and the changing. Of course what is unchanging will win."

The mind of "nothing" is the mind of meditative concentration. This "no-mind" is the best way to deal with deluded thoughts, for no-mind is a mind that is unshakable. When we use this no-mind we see that when we have the chance to be rich or famous it is the best time to do good deeds, be generous, and cultivate the bodhisattva path. When we face problems and suffering it is the best time to develop our body and mind and build our resolve the best we can. The world is filled with trials and tribulation, and each is an opportunity to become detached from worldly illusions. Without craving for or attachment to anything in the world one will remain unmoved by the eight winds of gain, loss, defamation, honor, praise, ridicule, sorrow, and joy. This is the power of meditative concentration

The Powers of the Mind

Our bodies need power before they can shoulder a heavy load, and in the same way our mind needs power to be able to resist the various hardships of life. But how can we make our mind powerful?

The Buddhist sutras say there are four kinds of power we must possess. The first of these is the power of understanding. This means the power to understand questions thoroughly. When something is completely understood it is easy to put into practice, and by developing our power of understanding we enhance our practice.

Second is the power of enjoyment. This kind of power gives us an optimistic character. When we read a book, we should fully enjoy our reading. Likewise, when we work we should enjoy our work, when we serve others we should enjoy our service, and when we give we should enjoy our generosity.

Next is the power of rest. There is a Chinese saying that goes, "Rest to go farther." Sometimes we must rest after we have carried our burdens a long while so that our strength can be restored.

The final power is the power of contemplation, which is the work of meditative concentration. With meditative concentration the mind is not easily changed by outside circumstances. When our minds cannot be changed in this way we are instead able to change these circumstances, and this gives the mind power.

Meditative concentration is quite miraculous. Once it is developed things seem lively and natural. Daily life develops a sense of clarity, and you no longer worry about material concerns. The whole world is filled with a sense of vitality that can repair the disorder of modern people's lives. Meditative concentration can transform delusion into enlightenment, false ideas into correct understanding, what is small into what is great, and suffering into happiness.

The Bliss of Meditative Concentration

People will follow their sense organs to whatever makes them happy. In actuality, a wellspring of happiness can be found whenever a Chan practitioner closes his or her eyes.

After the Buddha's cousin Prince Bhadrika joined the monastic order he was deep in meditation with two other monastics when they all shouted at once, "Such bliss! Such bliss!"

When the Buddha heard of this, he asked Bhadrika, "Just now you were shouting, 'Such bliss! Such bliss!' What made you so happy?"

Bhadrika replied, "Lord Buddha, I think about how I used to live deep inside a high-walled palace, where each day I would eat the finest delicacies and be dressed in fine silks and brocades, and where many guards protected me day and night, but I still felt fear. It felt as if someone was coming to assassinate me, and I lived each day with these uneasy feelings. Now that I have joined the monastic order and practice meditation, though my food is plain and simple it is satisfying and tastes wonderful. Though I reside amid the trees of the forest, I feel safe, secure, and free. I could not help but call out in joy."

What Bhadrika experienced was the bliss of meditative concentration. The enjoyment that comes from meditation is not the same as the happiness of the five desires or the six sense objects. One who meditates enjoys the bliss of meditative concentration and the joy of the Dharma that cannot be changed by time or space. The bliss of meditative concentration is unlike anything else in the world.

Some people believe that romantic love will make them happiest, but romantic love is like a flower blossom: as beautiful and fragrant as it may be, it cannot last long. Romantic love is like biting into a persimmon, for though it has some sweetness, it carries with it a sour, tart, and bitter taste. Sometimes romantic love burns like fire, making you giddy and unable to control yourself, when at other times love is as cold as ice, and gets tangled up with hate such that your life feels meaningless.

Some say that it is not necessary to have romantic love, and that money makes them happy. But money is not all-powerful. Money can buy all the rich delicacies of the land and seas, but it cannot buy a healthy appetite. Money can buy high-class cosmetics and beautiful, stylish clothes, but it cannot buy an elegant personality. Money can buy an expensive bed, but it cannot buy restful sleep. Money can buy thousands of books, but it cannot buy wisdom. Money can buy power, but it cannot buy respect.

All the wealth in the world is subject to the five causes of loss: fire, flood, corrupt governments, robbers, and wayward children. Fame and glory are as illusory as a dream, and wealth and honor are as ephemeral as a winter frost. Romantic love, money, fame, position, and power will not last, and cannot bring true happiness. True happiness comes from having meditative concentration in your everyday life.

The Wisdom of Meditative Concentration

When learning about Buddhism, some people may read the Buddhist sutras or listen to some teachings, but they may not have much insight into the Dharma. As soon as something comes up they feel confused and are filled with delusion. One may seem enlightened in speech, but be deluded when facing life's circumstances. This is why Buddhism emphasizes both understanding and practice. It is not enough to speak like an enlightened person, one must have a mind that is unshakable in all circumstances. To practice meditation and become enlightened one must have an unshakable mind. This is extremely important.

When you do not know enough about yourself your mind cannot feel independent. You will be easily influenced by external circumstances: a single word of praise will make you glow with pride, while an ill spoken word will stir resentment and anger. When this happens your joy, happiness, sorrow, and suffering is totally under the control of others. In a sense, you have already completely lost yourself.

In this world, as long as we have the distinction between "you" and "I" there will be duality, and we will not have emptiness. Whenever there is a distinction between ordinary beings and Buddhas there can be no equality. Meditation seeks to create equality where there is duality, and unification where there is differentiation. This is the wisdom of meditative concentration.

The wisdom of meditative concentration has the wondrous ability to illuminate the whole universe. Having meditation as a part of our daily life can have a profound and extraordinary effect upon us. Even in times of turmoil and upheaval, it can enable us to face life's hardships and remain composed by reducing our afflictions. With the wisdom of meditative concentration we can remain unaffected by right and wrong, advantage and disadvantage, gain and loss, honor and disgrace, even when dealing with hardships, stress, setbacks, and disappointments.

The *Suramgama Sutra* says, "If one is able to change things, then one is the same as the Tathagata." Putting effort into developing meditative concentration means being unfazed by external circumstances, letting everything go, and being concerned about nothing. After that, the world is no longer the same.

I have spent more than sixty years of my life as a monastic, having first joined the monastic order at the age of twelve. When I was young I received a traditional monastic education where we were trained to neither listen to nor see any outside thing. This was an education of beating and scolding where the unreasonable had to be accepted as reasonable, and the inhumane as humane. Either way, I happily accepted all of it, knowing that it was simply a matter of course, for I had no doubts, no resentment, and no sense of unfairness. Even after I formally began my Dharma teaching career at the age of twenty, there was no end to the discrimination, repression, misunderstanding, defamation, and injury I suffered for many years. At times I did feel anger and resentment, and felt hampered by instances of honor, disgrace, praise, or blame. But having been trained and nurtured by Buddhism for more than sixty years now, I no longer treat gain, loss, success, or failure that seriously any more. My heart is free of resentment and feelings of unfairness, and I am no longer bothered by praise, blame, honor, disgrace, or the worries of life and death. When I think about the world and its ideas and consider what is right, wrong, good, or bad, I feel like I have returned to my childhood and see everything as a matter of course.

This world is impermanent. You may not want the world to change, but that is impossible. However, as long as your mind remains unchanged by external circumstances, you will be fine. This world is filled with doubt and confusion about ourselves and others, what is right and wrong or good and bad, and what exists or does not exist. It is difficult to change the world to be the way you want. Changing yourself is the best approach.

Once there was a young man who had just gotten married and he would tell everyone he met how wonderful married life was.

Every day after work, he came home and his wife would bring him his slippers, while his little dog would run around, barking affectionately. But, after three years, things had changed. Now when he came home each day, it was not his wife who brought him his slippers, it was his little dog who came holding them in his mouth; and it was not his little dog who ran around barking, instead it was his wife who kept prattling on incessantly. The man felt extremely depressed and helpless, so he went to the temple to talk with a Buddhist master.

The Buddhist master listened to the young man's story and said, "Very good! You should be so happy! You still have slippers to wear and are greeted with sounds just as before. Your life hasn't changed at all. Besides, no matter how your circumstances change, as long as your mind does not change, you will be fine."

To have a mind that can remain unaltered by circumstances is the power of meditative concentration. When you cross your legs and close your eyes, even if you don't achieve some state of deep meditative concentration or attain enlightenment, the bliss of meditative concentration will bubble up from your heart. If you can take the next step and use your meditation to expand your capacity to give, then even if you suffer some small loss or are wronged in some small way, you can still feel okay about it.

Meditative Concentration and Compassion

The life of a Chan practitioner is one of great compassion. It is a life where one liberates the world by taking on the hardships of living beings. Practicing meditation is not just about enjoying the bliss of meditative concentration or the joy of the Dharma. Instead one should cherish all living beings, and seek to constantly refine oneself.

Once, Chan Master Zhaozhou Congshen asked Chan Master Nanquan Puyuan, "Where will you go in the future?"

Nanquan answered saying, "I will seek rebirth as an ox in the household of a state councilor."

Chan practitioners do not practice for their sake alone. We must treat living beings with the great compassion and zeal of a bodhisattva, not be selfish and only wish to liberate ourselves. We must look inside ourselves and see our faults, renew ourselves through constant purification, and practice such that we seek nothing outside ourselves, turning away from the internal and the external.

We must neither abide in *samsara* nor *nirvana*. Not abiding in *samsara* means using wisdom to transcend the cycle of rebirth, and not abiding in *nirvana* means using compassion to serve all living beings. When practicing meditation, we cannot ignore upholding the precepts or cultivating compassion. Upholding the precepts purifies the body and mind and makes it easier to develop meditative concentration. Cultivating compassion allows us to feel empathy, so our meditation does not become like a dead piece of wood.

When we practice meditation, if we place too much emphasis on compassion alone it becomes a misuse of compassion, and will

 ## *Samsara: The Cycle of Rebirth*

Samsara is a Sanskrit word that means "wandering," and refers to the living beings who wander through life only to die and be reborn again in another life. *Samsara* has no beginning and, without the liberating wisdom of the Buddhist teachings, no end.

create obstacles for us instead. If we place too much emphasis on wisdom, the tranquility of our meditative concentration becomes vacant and stagnant, and we become cold and callous. To cultivate the Middle Way, compassion and wisdom must be practiced together.

Some people may think that monastics renounce the secular world and live a reserved life amid oil lamps and ancient Buddhas, and that it is a negative, pessimistic life that is withdrawn from the world. In reality, the only things a monastic renounces are the illusions of the world. They let go of scheming for their own advantage and live life in a more liberated, real, and positive way. Renunciation does not mean running away from something, but going forth courageously and actively seeking out the truth. One cannot do anything authentically without first renouncing and seeing things clearly. One must have a supramundane mind that resolves to attain enlightenment before one can do the compassionate work of the mundane world.

A Chan practitioner must not indulge in the bliss of meditative concentration, but generate the aspiration to attain enlightenment and liberate all living beings so that they can share the joy of the Dharma. As the *Diamond Sutra* says, "All sentient beings, whether they are born from eggs, born from a womb, born in moisture, or born from transformation; whether they are with form or without form; whether they are with perception, without perception, or are neither with perception nor without perception; I will cause them all to enter *nirvana* without remainder, liberating them." This is the only way to be a Chan practitioner of Humanistic Buddhism.

The Four Means of Embracing

A Humanistic Buddhist should practice the bodhisattva's four means of embracing.

- *Giving* material things, fearlessness, and the Dharma as needed by living beings, so that they are free from worry and despair.
- *Kind words* that praise and encourage living beings to increase their faith.
- *Empathy* when helping others, so that we understand the plight of living beings, and can help them through their problems together, so that they faithfully accept the teachings.
- *Altruism* that attends to the needs of living beings so that they can be introduced to the wisdom of the Buddhas.

Chan and Humanistic Buddhism

In Humanistic Buddhism a Chan mind is a pure mind. True Chan practitioners are unaffected by power, position, emotion, or the cycle of rebirth. For Chan practitioners to develop meditative concentration they need the training, experience, and wisdom of daily life. They must be able to pick things up and put them down, allowing what comes to come and what goes to go. Living day to day like this is to live a life of wisdom, and is one of the wondrous uses of meditative concentration.

Chan can give us enlightenment and clear understanding. It eliminates ignorance, so that we can appreciate how beautiful life really is. The enlightened mind is like a lake with clear water: without the waves of affliction, you can see all the way to the bottom. Chan is wisdom and intelligence; it is flexibility, humor, and compassion. Chan can make our delusion and afflictions disappear.

With a Chan sense of humor and composure an embarrassing word, an awkward situation, or an unhappy past event can vanish completely.

Chan is the extra bit of flavor that makes life more wonderful. Chan is like a bright light in the darkened room of our mind that naturally reveals our wisdom. Chan is what allows us to freely observe other people, our own minds, and external circumstances; it lets us act with proper conduct, express ourselves correctly, and be free from deluded thoughts. Chan allows us to be content with simplicity, joyful with tranquility, and cherish our blessings. With Chan we have no demands, but only persevere diligently towards developing meditative concentration and wisdom. Chan allows us to let go of things with laughter, see through everything without obstruction, and attain liberation and freedom.

With Chan time is limitless, space is boundless, and there is no distinction between oneself and others. Eternity exists in an instant, and a single thought contains the whole universe. You may worry that an enlightened Chan practitioner is getting on in years, but they will tell you they have no time to grow old. You may want them to travel and see the sights, but they will tell you that the dharma realm[12] is within the mind.

In reality, internal and external are one. A Chan practitioner sees the afflictions of the world as flowing water, and visualizes the hardships of human life as *nirvana*. With Chan, even a single moment can be enjoyed for a lifetime and never be exhausted. The mind of a Chan practitioner contains the entire universe. The life of a Chan practitioner is intimately connected with nature. Nature's mountains, rivers, trees, flowers, and grass, its rain, dew, and gentle breezes, as well as the sun, moon, and stars are a wealth we all share. Only by being one with nature can there be eternal wealth.

Meditation for Everyone

Actually, meditative concentration does not belong only to a handful of Chan practitioners; it belongs to the world. Meditation is like the brightness of the full moon. The full moon in the sky is bright without making a showy display; it is soft and unpretentious. The moon shines over all the mountains and rivers equally, and shows its perfect fullness while hiding nothing.

Meditative concentration is our intrinsic nature. The Buddha said, "All sentient beings have Buddha nature." Each of us carries with us the treasure of Buddha nature. Most people do not recognize this treasure and instead fill their days chasing after what they see, hear, feel, and know, pursuing wealth and position, and creating attachments to the five desires and the six sense objects. Their true mind is cast among the six realms of existence, where they will be reborn again and again.

 The Six Realms of Existence

In Buddhism, the desire realm is said to be made up of six different realms of existence. Depending on our karma we can be reborn in any of these six realms for a time, though our existence there is only temporary. Each realm is populated by different kinds of beings, not all of which can be seen by those in the human realm. The six realms of existence are:

1. Heaven
2. The Realm of Asuras[13]
3. The Realm of Human Beings
4. The Realm of Animals
5. The Realm of Hungry Ghosts
6. Hell

Fortunately, the intrinsic nature of the true mind neither arises nor ceases, and does not increase or decrease. No matter how long we are lost in the cycle of rebirth our true mind remains unborn and undying. There will come a day when we will have meditative concentration's wisdom of awakening and contemplation so that what we see, hear, know, and feel will be unaffected by external circumstances. We will then be able to transform the ordinary into the sagely, and achieve the following:

1. *Transform the ordinary world of differences into the sagely world of equality.*
Ordinary people understand the world as being full of differentiation. For a sage, the world is all about equality. In Buddhism there is an old saying, "Living beings and Buddhas are equal. Oneself and other are equal. Existence and non-existence are equal. Sages and ordinary people are equal." A world with equality is a world that is true and beautiful.

2. *Transform the ordinary world of turmoil into the sagely world of tranquility.*
The world of ordinary people is contaminated by material desire, and is thus full of commotion and rushing about. Conversely, sages seek the bliss of meditative concentration and the joy of the Dharma: a world that is tranquil and free of turmoil. If we can settle our minds and bodies into tranquility we can then truly know the world.

3. *Transform the ordinary world of arising and ceasing into the sagely world of nirvana.*
The ordinary world has arising and ceasing, and thus is impermanent. Beings are born, grow old, become sick, and

die, while matter arises, abides, changes, and ceases. If we can distinguish things well and put an end to the distinctions of time and space, ourselves and others, and birth and death we will arrive at the sage's world of *nirvana* and be able to know the true reality of all phenomena.

4. Transform the ordinary world of defilement into the sagely world of purity.

This world is filled with killing, stealing, sexual misconduct, and lying. If we have the wisdom of meditative concentration, we can be sure our bodies will not kill, steal, or commit sexual misconduct; our speech will be free of lies, harsh words, duplicity, and flattery; and our minds will have no greed, anger, or ignorance. We can then transform the ordinary world of defilement into the sagely world of purity, for only that is the real world.

5. Transform the ordinary world of imperfection into the sagely world of perfection.

The ordinary world is made up of parts. Part of the time it is day and part of the time it is night. Part of the population is male and part is female, part of it is made up of good people and part is made up of bad people. Part of the world is the Buddha's and part is Mara's.[14] The ordinary world is full of imperfection, but if we can develop meditative concentration we can perfect our human conduct, perfect our merit and wisdom, and perfect our practice. Then we will transform this world into the sagely world of perfection that is permanent, blissful, pure, and has an inherent self.

6. *Transform the ordinary world of suffering into the sagely world of happiness.*

The ordinary world is filled with all kinds of sadness and suffering: birth, old age, sickness, death, being apart from those we love, being with those we dislike, not getting what we want, and the intense suffering of the five aggregates. If we realize our Buddha nature, then we can join the sages and ascend to a world of happiness full of the bliss of meditative concentration and the joy of the Dharma.

The *Avatamsaka Sutra* says, "Always enjoy the practice of gentleness and patience; find your repose in the four immeasurables of loving kindness, compassion, joy, and equanimity." If we possess the power of meditative concentration, we can find peace in the truth and will no longer be moved by wealth, passion, fame, slander, suffering, hardship, profit, or anger.

No matter how good or bad the world becomes, if the mind remains unshakable then, even if we find our bodies mired in mud, we can still grow into a pure lotus. What is most important in life is to find peace in the tranquility of meditative concentration, so that we can live as Chan practitioners. This is the effect of meditative concentration on life: living life at its happiest.

Chapter Nine

Opening the Door of Prajna
The Causes of Wisdom

What is Prajna?

M OST RELIGIONS EMPHASIZE faith and compassion, only Buddhism emphasizes reason and the pursuit of wisdom. Buddhism recognizes that we can only distinguish right from wrong and truth from falsehood by developing wisdom. Only by developing wisdom can we eliminate affliction, and liberate ourselves and others.

Buddhism seeks to develop a special kind of wisdom that Buddhists call *prajna*. *Prajna* is a Sanskrit word which literally means "wisdom," but in practice it refers to a profound understanding of reality. For this reason, since Buddhism's beginnings in India, the word "prajna" has usually remained untranslated out of respect for the unique quality of this kind of wisdom. Prajna is not information, knowledge, or philosophy, but is the wisdom of life and the universe that goes beyond definitions and duality.

As mentioned previously, when the Buddha became enlightened he declared that all sentient beings have Buddha nature. This means that ordinary beings are the same as the Buddha, for they all posses the capacity to become Buddhas. Why then did the Buddha become enlightened and realize Buddhahood so long ago while we are still journeying through the cycle of rebirth? This is because we have not uncovered our intrinsic prajna nature. Just as the moon is obscured by clouds in the sky, the prajna of ordinary people is obscured. If we can uncover our intrinsic prajna nature and see our original face, then we can live in this world not only with wealth and honor, but with unsurpassed freedom and liberty.

The Buddha spent forty-nine years teaching the Dharma. Twenty-two of those years were dedicated exclusively to teachings on prajna, more than any other single topic. These teachings reveal our original face, and the Buddhist view on human life and the universe.

Prajna is the intrinsic nature of all living beings. With prajna there is no duality between living beings and Buddhas, or between ourselves and other people. The sutras say, "Within the absolute, true reality the provisional names for sentient beings and Buddhas no longer apply. Within the nature of equality, the forms of self and other are no longer present."

A Verse on Prajna

There is no metaphor for prajna;
Ordinary beings, sravakas, and pratyekabuddhas cannot
*   comprehend it;*
Even bodhisattvas of equal enlightenment are unable to
*   know it;*
Only the Buddha, the world-honored one, can do so.

Right View

Prajna is the enlightened state of a Buddha. It fundamentally cannot be described, nor can it easily be discussed. To try to explain prajna, I have broken it down into four levels, each of which has its own features. The first level is the prajna of right view, the second is the prajna of dependent origination, the third is the prajna of emptiness, and the fourth is the true prajna of the Buddha.

The first level of prajna is right view. Superficially, prajna means wisdom, though there are key differences. Prajna is perfect, where wisdom can sometimes be flawed, and lead to delusion. Prajna is always beneficial, while a smart person with a lot of wisdom might use that wisdom to outsmart themselves. Prajna is everlasting; it is the way things are.

Prajna can be quite difficult to explain, but this analogy is a good place to start: Imagine taking photographs of an outdoor scene. By using a camera we can take beautiful pictures of the mountains, rivers, and grass, but we must adjust the focus and aperture so that the pictures appear sharp. Prajna is like correctly adjusting the camera so we can see all phenomena clearly.

To have right view is to see things correctly, turn away from all wrong views, and truly understand cause and effect on a mundane and supramundane level. There are many Buddhist teachings which talk about ways to understand reality, such as the teachings on karma, impermanence, emptiness, the Three Dharma Seals, the Four Noble Truths, and the Twelve Links of Dependent Origination. Each of these teachings is part of what it means to have right view.

An individual's ideas and principles can influence his or her entire life, and thus it is very important that these principles are correct. Some Buddhists encounter injustice or hardship and

completely lose faith in the Way and give up. These people voice
all sorts of complaints against Buddhism, and blame the Buddhas
and bodhisattvas for not protecting them. This is not right view.
Right view means having such faith in the truth of your principles
that they cannot be shaken by any difficulty you may encounter.
Rather than weakening it, adversity should strengthen our faith,
cause us to hold fast to our principles, and motivate us to protect
the common good and declare the truth fearlessly.

We must clearly understand that the world contains both good
and bad, that karma and the effects of karma exist, that there are
past lives and future lives, and that there are both ordinary people
and noble sages. We must know what is virtuous and non-virtuous;
what is sacred and profane; what is past, present, and future; and
what are the effects of karma. Only through this understanding
can we guard our actions, speech, and thoughts, do only what is
wholesome, and refrain from what is unwholesome so that we are
not reborn as animals, hungry ghosts, or in hell.

Dependent Origination

The next level of prajna is known by sravakas, pratyekabuddhas,[15]
and arhats. These are three kinds of beings who have attained a
high level of cultivation, and who are a step above ordinary people.
Because of this, they have a superior understanding of life, the
universe, and all phenomena. This level of prajna is characterized
by an understanding of "dependent origination." Dependent
origination is a fundamental Buddhist teaching and describes
how all things in the world arise due to causes and conditions
and cease when the proper conditions are no longer present.
Dependent origination is one of the features that makes Buddhism
different from all other religions. Dependent origination explains

that nothing in the world comes from nowhere, nor can anything exist by itself, for all things exist in reliance upon many causes and conditions and these causes and conditions too rely upon other causes and conditions.

This complex set of interdependent relationships explains the existence of the universe, the genesis of life, and the non-duality of the Middle Way. This teaching is the very thing that the Buddha realized the night of his awakening, when he gazed up at the stars— the doctrine of dependent origination.

Since all things arise due to causes and conditions, for us to live a happy life we must create good causes and conditions. If we wish to have good relationships with other people, we must create connections with them so that we can meet again in the future.

When we are faced with the negative effects of past karma we can understand the causes and conditions that led to our current outcome. The point, of course, is not to stubbornly become obsessed with karma or to go around blaming everyone but ourselves. This only needlessly entangles us in more layers of affliction. Instead, understanding the relationship between dependent origination and karma allows us to cultivate good conditions and form good connections with other people.

Emptiness

The next level of prajna is experienced by bodhisattvas, and it is called "emptiness." When many people hear the word "emptiness" they think of nothingness, but that is not at all what emptiness means. Emptiness is a profound philosophical concept in Mahayana Buddhism, and when used in that context the meaning of "emptiness" is much closer to infinity than nothingness.

Existence is only possible because of emptiness. There must be empty space first before it can contain all the myriad forms of life in the universe. If there is no empty space in a wallet it cannot hold anything. If a house has no empty space, no one can live in it. If our nostrils have no empty space we cannot even breathe!

By understanding the nature of emptiness we can understand the truth of the universe and of life itself. Emptiness is how we can discover the truth of the inherent non-existence of all things.

What exactly is emptiness? Emptiness is dependent origination, right view, non-duality, and prajna itself. Emptiness is limitless, like the number zero in mathematics. If you put a "0" after a "1," it becomes "10." If you place another "0" after that, it becomes "100," and with one more it becomes "1000." You can keep adding zeros forever until you reach astronomical figures.

Emptiness is all inclusive and ever expanding. It is like reciting the name of Amitabha Buddha. When I say "Amitofo" it can have an infinite number of meanings. When you give me something I say "Amitofo" as an expression of gratitude. If you get promoted or become rich I say "Amitofo" to wish you well. When someone passes away I say "Amitofo" to express my condolences. "Amitofo" is truth, just as emptiness is truth. "Amitofo" is all of existence, for it can be whatever you say it is. In the same way, emptiness is all of existence, for it can be whatever you like it to be.

All of existence is born from the emptiness of the universe, just as all things on earth rely on the air to breathe. Existence is built out of emptiness. The relationship between emptiness and existence is like that of an open palm and a fist: when you close your palm it becomes a fist, and opening your fist reveals your palm. In the same way, emptiness becomes existence through the coming together of causes and conditions, and existence reverts to emptiness when these causes and conditions disperse. Emptiness and existence arise and cease in this way in an unending process of change. When you understand the relationship between emptiness and existence, you will see that they are different, yet the same; the same, and yet different.

The relationship between emptiness and existence is like the process of making gold jewelry. Ore has to be mined, refined, and shipped to a factory to become gold. The gold is then sold to a jewelry shop where it is made into all kinds of rings, earrings, necklaces, and bracelets. Though the gold has gone through many changes during this process, the substance of the gold itself never really changes. Emptiness is like gold, and existence is like all the beautiful things that can be made from gold. There is only one kind of emptiness, while there are many kinds of existence. Emptiness is the substance, while existence is its appearance.

Emptiness is like a stern father, while existence is like a kind mother. Father and mother join together to give birth to us, just as emptiness and existence harmonize together to create all phenomena. This is why the *Heart Sutra* says, "Emptiness is form, form is emptiness."

All phenomena arise due to dependent origination, and because of this they are empty and lack intrinsic nature. They arise only temporarily and then pass into extinction. This temporary existence that arises through dependent origination is but an appearance. In reality, all phenomena are inherently empty, and thus they neither arise nor pass into extinction. All phenomena are empty due to dependent origination, yet it is because of their empty nature that they are able to arise through dependent origination.

Emptiness occupies an important position is Buddhist thought, for it is a truth that cannot be invalidated. The doctrine of emptiness has greatly contributed to humanity, for an understanding of emptiness allows us to see through delusion and construct existence from within emptiness. A worldview based on emptiness can refine and improve the value of human life.

The integration of emptiness and existence is known as the "Middle Way." This kind of wisdom allows us to have direct insight into true reality. With this understanding we can know that, whatever comes up, it has not happened for some random reason but has occurred due to universal principles. Likewise, when we experience the results of our karma, we can know that every effect has a cause. Since we understand cause and effect we will never blame anyone other than ourselves and know that we can only seek answers and resolve our problems by looking into their fundamental causes.

The Buddha's Prajna

The *Treatise on the Perfection of Great Wisdom* states, "The perfection of prajna is the true reality of all phenomena that cannot be negated or destroyed." With prajna one can realize the inherent emptiness of all phenomena that arises from dependent origination and thus become a Buddha. Prajna is the "cause" of enlightenment.

Prajna is the complete and bright wisdom of enlightenment, and is the way that all Buddhas and bodhisattvas realize the true reality of all phenomena. It is a kind of wisdom which is pure and without distinctions that turns away from all confused and deluded thoughts. It is a kind of wisdom that is true and formless, and allows us to know that all phenomena are inherently empty and that there is fundamentally nothing to attain.

An ordinary person who has right knowledge and right view can be said, to a certain extent, to have developed prajna. That being said, prajna can only truly be realized by becoming a Buddha. That is why the *Lotus Sutra* says, "Only between one Buddha and another Buddha can the true reality of all phenomena be fathomed." The *Treatise on the Perfection of Great Wisdom* also says, "Among all the various kinds of wisdom, prajna is foremost, unsurpassed, incomparable, unequaled, and superior beyond all others."

Prajna is the Buddha's level of wisdom. It is the state of non-duality that encompasses both essence and appearance. When the Buddha sat beneath the bodhi tree and looked up at the stars, he realized the dependent origination of prajna. In essence, prajna is the root of all phenomena, the nature of all beings, and our endless life. The form of prajna is that of a beautiful flower, a shining light, a compassionate mother, and a rescue boat. The function of prajna is the ability to use wisdom to humorously and ingeniously solve problems. An individual with prajna is able to remain open-minded and can comprehend and perceive all matters. He or she can transcend the distinctions of self and other, right and wrong, existence and non-existence, and good and bad.

In Buddhism, there is a bodhisattva named Ksitigarbha who made the great vow to go into the hell realm so that he could liberate all the living beings in hell. Having heard this story, one might ask the question: does Ksitigarbha Bodhisattva suffer in hell? No, he does not, because of his prajna. He does not suffer in the same way that the parents in a poor family do not suffer from all the hardships they must endure to raise their children: because of compassion. Compassion and motherly love are prajna.

Prison officers do not suffer if they maintain their mission of service, but they will suffer if they use their authority to abuse others. If convicts in prison feel repentant and take every opportunity to reflect and reform they will not suffer, but they will suffer if they feel dissatisfied and voice their grievances and resentments. The difference between suffering and not suffering is all in the mind.

Your state of mind can also show whether prajna is present or not. With prajna, you can handle anything that happens and everything is seen with an ordinary mind that is natural and simple. When Chan Master Zhitong became enlightened by realizing that "female practitioners are originally women," that was prajna, for with prajna one can see the Dharma in common, ordinary things.

With prajna one can know suffering and the end of suffering by contemplating emptiness. Most people spend their days doing nothing but pursuing the six sense objects, and thus they live in a deluded and unreal world. They easily fall prey to inverted thinking which leads to confusion and creates karma, causing such people to endlessly journey through the cycle of rebirth. Life without prajna lacks right view, and one becomes easily manipulated by the afflictions of external circumstances. However, with prajna you can develop the light of intrinsic nature, come to know your real life, and cross over from the near shore of *samsara* to the far shore of *nirvana*.

Prajna and the Six Perfections

Prajna has the wondrous use of allowing us to become enlightened to the true reality of all phenomena. However, the most important way for each of us to use prajna is as the basis to develop the six perfections. With prajna we can give joyfully without any thought of being generous, be moral without any attachment to the forms of the precepts, be patient by abandoning the attachment to the self, be diligent without a sense of pride, and attain meditative

The Six Perfections

The six perfections are the six things that bodhisattvas seek to perfect in order to realize the bodhisattva path and become Buddhas. They are:

- The perfection of giving
- The perfection of morality
- The perfection of patience
- The perfection of diligence
- The perfection of meditative concentration
- The perfection of prajna

concentration without being captivated by any meditative state. That is why the sutras say that "Prajna is the guide and the other five perfections follow it. Without prajna, the other five perfections are blind."

Consider, for example, the perfection of giving. There are many charitable organizations in the world, and many ordinary people who act generously. However, if this generosity lacks prajna, it is not the ultimate form of giving. With prajna, one can see that the person who gives, the one who receives, and the gift itself are all empty and the distinctions between giver and recipient are eliminated. This kind of giving stands apart from the mundane world, and is different from worldly forms of giving. In the same way, without prajna, our morality cannot truly benefit all living beings. Without prajna, our patience cannot encompass the non-arising of all phenomena. Without prajna, we cannot have the diligence to constantly put forth effort. Without prajna, our meditative concentration will never lead us to enlightenment.

Prajna is what allows us to make the other five qualities into perfections. Without prajna, giving only secures a lifetime of honor, but after this life one will suffer from other unwholesome deeds. Without prajna, morality can lead to temporary rebirth in a higher realm, but eventually one will sink down into hell. Without prajna, patience can give us a pleasant appearance but not the tranquil patience of *nirvana*. Without prajna, diligence can help us to generate merit, but cannot lead us to the ocean of true permanence. Without prajna, our meditative concentration can only lead us to the first four dhyana states, but not beyond that. Without prajna, some afflictions remain, and the merit will slowly drain away from our good deeds like water leaking from a broken cup. Without prajna, all the Buddha's teachings are mundane teachings, for they only truly become the Dharma when there is prajna.

The Cultivation of Prajna

The great function of prajna is to lead all of the practices of the six perfections into the ocean of wisdom. Prajna is the basis for the six perfections and the source of all wholesome teachings. It can move us beyond the sea of *samsara* and deliver us to the other shore of enlightenment, and is called the "mother of all Buddhas." There are three kinds of prajna:

The Prajna of True Reality

This is the fundamental substance of prajna and is possessed by all living beings. With this type of prajna, all illusions are eliminated. It is the Buddha's prajna, the true nature of prajna, and is the understanding of the general and specific characteristics of all phenomena.

The Prajna of Contemplation
This type of prajna is capable of contemplating true reality and seeing that all phenomena are without intrinsic nature. It is the prajna of sravakas and pratyekabuddhas, and is the understanding of the general characteristics of all phenomena.

The Prajna of Skillful Means
This type of prajna skillfully distinguishes all phenomena. It is the prajna of bodhisattvas, and is the understanding of the specific characteristics of all phenomena.

The prajna of skillful means logically judges the distinctive characteristics of all phenomena, while the prajna of contemplation directly sees the true reality of all phenomena. These two kinds of prajna emanate from the prajna of true reality, which is possessed by all living beings.

Such wisdom is developed by diligently studying the Dharma and advancing from the simple to the profound step-by-step. This wisdom can be developed by being close to good Dharma friends, listening to Dharma talks, or reading from the Buddhist sutras. By listening, one can attain wisdom by believing and understanding the meaning of the words.

Wisdom can also be gained through thinking about the Buddhist teachings, deeply pondering them, and reviewing their meaning until one comes to a profound understanding of the truth. To gain wisdom by thinking about the Buddhist teachings it is important that we rely on the proper things. The Buddha advised us to rely on four things when learning his teachings, and called them the "Four Reliances." They are:

- Rely on the Dharma, not on an individual teacher.
- Rely on the meaning, not on the words.
- Rely on the ultimate truth, not on relative truth.
- Rely on wisdom, not on knowledge.

If we rely on these four things, we will be able to experience the Buddha's teachings correctly and realize the ultimate meaning of the teachings.

Wisdom can also be gained through practice. After we have come to an understanding of the teachings through listening to and thinking about them we must diligently put them into practice and develop contemplative wisdom. Through listening, thinking, and practicing one can attain true prajna that has no duality between subject and object. In this way, one is able to abandon affliction and attain liberation.

Prajna is like a beacon that exposes the truth of all phenomena and shows the correct path to take in life. Prajna is not external knowledge; but is the pure, bright nature of all living beings, and their original face. Each person has his or her own Buddha nature, and thus Huineng, the Sixth Patriarch of the Chan School, said "All prajna wisdom arises from intrinsic nature." One who has realized his intrinsic nature has attained prajna.

That being said, Huineng also cautioned us that, "People talk about prajna all day long without getting to know the prajna within their intrinsic nature." Everyone has a mind, but most people only pay attention to the physical, and are thus full of delusion and discrimination. They ignore their true mind, which is the mind of prajna. With prajna the whole universe is contained within the mind.

Prajna is a complex concept and is difficult to comprehend. It cannot be fully explained with language, but if we must try to speak of it, we can use the metaphor of the mirror:

Whether an individual is fat, thin, beautiful, or ugly, they can glance into a mirror, the mirror will reflect what is truly there, and the person will see their true appearance. In the same way, when Buddhist disciples practice reciting sutras, paying homage to the Buddha, or performing various works of merit, they must polish the mirror of the mind, for when the mind is pure, prajna will appear before them.

Even if we suffer criticism, slander, and abuse, with prajna we can look upon such experiences as dispelling future troubles. While suffering bitter setbacks, assaults, injustice, and insults, we can see them as indirect causes for something positive. These can turn into nutrients for our spiritual cultivation, which nourish the roots of the virtues that lead to enlightenment.

The Three Dharma Seals: Buddhist Truth

All of the world's religions feel that their own teachings are the truth. However, for something to really be true it must apply to all things universally and equally, and it must be eternal, certain, transcendent, and confirmable. For example, emptiness does not exist because someone happened to discover it; it has always existed. There is no "my emptiness" or "your emptiness," just the same emptiness that has been eternally and equally present in all things. Another example is the inevitability of death. Death is universal, certain, and eternal. It does not matter which continent you live on, death affects all people equally.

There is a Buddhist teaching called the "Three Dharma Seals." The Three Dharma Seals are laws of the universe and of human life that apply to all things universally and equally, and are eternal, certain, transcendent, and confirmable. They are called "seals," because they are used as seals of approval for the Buddhist teachings. We can know that a teaching is true if all Three Dharma Seals apply to it, and we can know that any teaching that lacks the Three Dharma Seals must be a false teaching. Even if something was spoken by the Buddha himself, if it goes against the Three Dharma Seals it cannot be a true teaching. Likewise, even if something was not directly spoken by the Buddha, if it is in accord with the Three Dharma Seals, it can be considered a true Buddhist teaching. The Three Dharma Seals are:

All Conditioned Phenomena Are Impermanent

Conditioned phenomena are those which come into this world through the combination of causes and conditions. Such phenomena are empty and are without an intrinsic nature: they arise when conditions come together and cease when those conditions disperse. Living beings are born, grow old, become sick, and die. Mountains, rivers, the planet earth, and all forms of matter in the universe arise, abide, change, and cease. Even thoughts are subject to arising, abiding, changing, and ceasing. All phenomena arise and pass into extinction from moment to moment, for they cannot linger for even a single instant. In the same way, the past is already gone, the future has yet to appear, and the present is arising and ceasing. Since phenomena are constantly shifting throughout the past, present, and future, it is said that all conditioned phenomena are impermanent.

All Phenomena Are without an Independent Self

"All phenomena are without an independent self" means that all conditioned and unconditioned phenomena lack any independent and unchanging substance or autonomy. This is because anything that can be called a "self" or an "inherent existence" must have a permanent and unchanging substance and be independent, self-determining, and unchanging. However, there is nothing in the world that is entirely separate from all other things, inherently existent, and self-determining, because all things arise depending on conditions. They exist when conditions come together and pass into extinction when conditions disperse. All things depend upon other things for existence and lack any substantial nature. Our bodies, wealth, fame, feelings, and everything in the world cannot exist forever. Sooner or later everything will abandon us, which is why "all phenomena are without an independent self."

Everything in this world is impermanent, and everything is without an independent self. If we understand the Law of Dependent Origination we will not become attached to mundane, impermanent phenomena that are without an independent self, but instead find our repose among supramundane phenomena that neither arise nor cease. Only in this way can we obtain a life of ultimate bliss.

Nirvana is Perfect Tranquility

The *Nirvana Sutra* states, "The cessation of all afflictions is called *nirvana.*" *Nirvana* refers to the cessation of greed, anger, ignorance, pride, and doubt, as well as the cessation of *samsara*, suffering, selfhood, and delusion. *Nirvana* is tranquility without outflows, and is a state of liberation filled with happiness, light, freedom, and comfort.

Buddhism sometimes gives the impression of being pessimistic and fleeing from ordinary life. This is because most people have a mistaken understanding of Buddhist principles like "suffering," "emptiness," and "impermanence." Some people may think that suffering and impermanence is all there is to Buddhism and do not realize the goal behind these teachings. Buddhism teaches us about suffering, emptiness, and impermanence so that we become weary of suffering, find joy in true happiness, and thus pursue the bliss of ultimate *nirvana*.

Instead of seeing them as pessimistic, we should see the Three Dharma Seals in the following way: there is only hope because of impermanence; living beings can only get along because they are without an independent self; and the ultimate state only exists because there is *nirvana*.

The Three Dharma Seals are not just the basis of the Buddhist teachings, they are the truth of the universe and of life itself. Truth is that which is fundamental and constant. It is important to remember that the Dharma, the truth of the way things are, exists on its own. Whether or not a Buddha appears in the world, the Dharma exists forever. The Buddha did not create this truth when he became enlightened; he was the one who discovered the truth. That is why the Buddha said, "Take refuge in yourself and in the Dharma, and nothing else."

The Buddhist Teachings Revisited

The Three Dharma Seals and dependent origination formed the philosophical basis of the teachings of Early Buddhism. The two doctrines are interrelated, and together they constitute the earliest foundational teachings of Buddhism. When these basic teachings are understood, one will naturally be in accord with the truth.

What are the truths of Buddhism? Broadly speaking, everything taught by the Buddha in his lifetime, everything contained within the Buddhist sutras, and everything that is in accord with reason are the truths of Buddhism. However, there is a small set of doctrines that are considered the basic doctrines of Buddhism. Several of these I have already mentioned, like the doctrine of karma and the Twelve Links of Dependent Origination, but I have collected them all here to give a complete picture of the Buddhist teachings:

1. Suffering

Suffering comes from our karma, our deluded thinking, our afflictions, and the five aggregates. Human life can seem like a big mass of suffering, but that is what drives us to find a way to extinguish suffering, transcend this world of misery, and liberate ourselves from this torment.

2. Impermanence

Part of the Three Dharma Seals, this is the truth that everything in this world, without exception, is changing all the time. Nothing remains constant, though this is not necessarily bad. Happiness is impermanent, but sadness is too. Only by transcending this world of impermanence can we attain eternal freedom.

3. Non-Self

Another one of the Dharma seals, this is the truth that all phenomena arise due to causes and conditions, and therefore they have no autonomous "self" that we can rely on. Nothing can exist independent of everything else.

4. Karma
Karma is everything we do, everything we say, and everything
we think. Whether it is wholesome or unwholesome, every act
of karma drives us act in new ways and generates more karma,
resulting in a never-ending karmic cycle.

5. Cause and Effect
Cause and effect is the truth of how all things in the universe
arise and cease. When the correct conditions are present, a
cause produces an effect, and this effect goes on to serve as a
cause for even more effects.

6. The Four Noble Truths
The four noble truths are (1) that there is a mass of suffering in
this world, (2) that this suffering is caused by ignorance, greed,
and anger, (3) that it is possible for this suffering to cease with
the tranquility of *nirvana*, and (4) that there is a path to the
cessation of suffering.

7. The Noble Eightfold Path
The Noble Eightfold Path is the path leading to the cessation of
suffering. The eight components are right view, right thought,
right speech, right action, right livelihood, right effort, right
mindfulness, and right meditative concentration.

8. The Twelve Links of Dependent Origination
The Twelve Links of Dependent Origination explain the causes
and effects that lead us through the cycle of rebirth. With a
single thought of **ignorance**, sentient beings create **mental
formations**. These formations generate karma, out of which

arises **consciousness**. When this consciousness enters the womb, **name and form** appear. This leads to the formation of the **six sense organs**, which come into **contact** with the outside world. With contact comes **feeling**, and then **craving** starts to arise for these feelings. Attachments form and this leads to **clinging**, and this clinging creates the karma of **becoming**, which has the karmic result of **birth**. As long as there is birth, there will be **aging and death**, and thus the cycle begins anew.

Transcendental Patience

Prajna allows us to truly know how life comes and goes, and it is only with prajna that we can have the strength to face the realities of life. To survive in this world we need both wisdom and power to alleviate our hardships and overcome adverse situations. Patience gives us both wisdom and strength.

Buddhism speaks of three levels of patience. The first is patience for life, which is a form of patience that acknowledges that conditions are a part of life. For example, to show up for work, we must get up early to catch the bus, and even if it is unpleasant it is a normal part of life. We must be patient with all kinds of discomfort like traffic jams, cold and heat, lack of sleep, differences of opinion, friendship, enmity, love, and hate. In order to move on with our lives, we must have patience for life.

The next level of patience is called patience for phenomena. Besides just maintaining our existence we must be able to live freely. We must be patient with greed, anger, ignorance, and prejudice by controlling ourselves, persuading ourselves, and changing ourselves. Having patience for phenomena means recognizing that all phenomena arise and cease. With this understanding we can allow the mind to find peace by no longer being affected by this arising and ceasing. Not only should we be unaffected by birth, old age, sickness, death, sadness, distress, fame, fortune, and the vagaries of human emotion, but we should be able to truly acknowledge, handle, and eliminate them.

The third and final level is patience for the non-arising of phenomena. This kind of patience is the highest level of patience and the understanding that phenomena fundamentally do not arise or cease. With patience for the non-arising of phenomena, there is really nothing to be patient or impatient about, since everything is simply just as it is.

When these three levels of patience are taken together, patience for life is the endurance needed to survive in the world, patience for phenomena transforms our consciousness into wisdom with the Buddhist teachings, and patience for the non-arising of phenomena is a state of freedom where we perceive all things as fundamentally neither arising nor ceasing. With this final level of patience, everywhere becomes a Pure Land,[16] and we can be completely free and at ease.

Right now, every group in the world, including academic circles, political circles, religious circles, and others, advocate for peace. However, most of these groups only advocate for peace with an eye towards their own self-interests. This is why we don't have peace. Only Buddhism, with its teachings on non-self, compassion, respect, and tolerance, and especially the equality that comes from prajna, is up to the challenge.

Without exception, everything that is noble, great, and profound, is based on equality. The sun shines everywhere on the earth equally, the air is for all of us to breathe equally, the flowing waters moisten all things equally, and the earth supports all living beings equally. The Buddha too understood equality, and stated that anyone from the four different castes of India became part of his family when they joined the monastic order. There must be the equality that comes from prajna before there can be any hope of peace for this world, or any ray of light for humanity. Only by laying a foundation of equality will there come a day when peace can truly be realized and not only be an empty slogan.

Chapter Ten

Skillful Knowledge
The Development of Wisdom

Knowledge and Openness

AS MENTIONED PREVIOUSLY, prajna is not the same as knowledge, and does not seek anything outside of intrinsic nature. However, to develop our intrinsic prajna nature we must listen, think, and practice. Learning Buddhism requires extensive study to fulfill the bodhisattva vow to learn infinite Dharmas so we can liberate all living beings. In ancient India all knowledge was categorized into the "Five Sciences," and a great practitioner was expected to have knowledge of all five. They are:

1. Grammar and Composition
2. Art and Mathematics
3. Medicine
4. Logic
5. Philosophy

The Four Universal Vows

The Four Universal Vows are made by bodhisattvas on their path to liberate themselves and others. Even today, many Buddhist practitioners make the Four Universal Vows as part of their practice. They are:
- Sentient beings are limitless, I vow to liberate them.
- Afflictions are endless, I vow to eradicate them.
- Dharmas are infinite, I vow to learn them.
- Buddhahood is supreme, I vow to attain it.

Though the Five Sciences cover a wide spectrum of knowledge, in today's multifaceted society these five can no longer supply what is needed. We are now in the Information Age where knowledge is everywhere. Knowledge may not be the same as wisdom, and it is certainly not the same as prajna, but it is the driving force of human life. Knowledge allows us to change our temperaments, understand the principles of life, and help advance our country and its citizens. Knowledge enhances commerce and industry, and it is through knowledge that science and philosophy are improved. Knowledge can inspire thought and transform the world.

For this reason Buddhism has never been wary of knowledge, but respects knowledge and has tolerance for other teachings. Buddhism lacks a sense of exclusivity and believes that its followers can benefit from learning about other teachings. For example, Laozi's teaching that "The Way that can be spoken is not the true Way" can broaden our horizons. There is also great benefit in Zhuangzi's teachings of unfettered exploration and being one with nature.

One famous exchange occurred when Hui Shi and Zhuangzi were walking by a river and Zhuangzi said, "See how the fishes dart around as they please? That is the happiness of fishes."

Hui Shi said to Zhuangzi, "You are not a fish, so how do you know the happiness of fishes?"

Zhuangzi replied, "You are not me, so how do you know that I do not know the happiness of fishes?"

The irrepressible spirit of Zhuangzi resembles Chan's style of being unrestrained by formalities. Humanistic Buddhist practitioners need not reject the doctrines of Laozi and Zhuangzi, nor any other teaching. We can equally accept Mencius's view that human nature is inherently good, Xunzi's view that human nature is inherently evil, and Mozi's teachings of universal love. Humanistic Buddhism does not reject any teaching, but sees other teachings as enriching and enlivening Buddhism.

It was because of a similar attitude of being open to all teachings that Buddhism was able to flourish in China. Before central Buddhist concepts became known throughout China, the philosophical terminology of other groups was used to express Buddhist ideas. During the Wei, Jin, and Northern and Southern dynasties Buddhism used the Lao Zhuang concept of "non-being" to explain the concept of "emptiness." It is for this same reason that Buddhism and Confucianism have long been commingled together.

In addition to the harmony in Chinese philosophy, Chinese literature found an affinity with Buddhism as well. Chinese culture has long appreciated literature, poetry, and the beauty of the written word, and the Buddhist sutras are filled with beautiful poetry and literary prose. The literary qualities of Buddhism made all of the many philosophical schools that were prominent during the "Hundred Schools of Thought" period sympathetic to Buddhism. As time went on Buddhism would continue to grow, bring Chan into the temples and monasteries, bring the Pure Land to the common people, and introduce the Consciousness-Only and Madhyamika schools to scholars.

The Integration of Knowledge

Buddhism is said to have eighty-four thousand methods of practice, and all of them lead to the Way. That being said, the Dharma can be divided into the two kinds of truth: ultimate truth and conventional truth. "Ultimate truth" is the foremost truth, the supreme truth, and contains the supramundane teachings. "Conventional truth" is also sometimes known as "relative truth," and is made up of the mundane teachings. All the Buddha's teachings are encompassed by these two truths.

To transform the world, the Dharma and secular learning must be applied together. The Dharma should not become too secular nor too otherworldly. If the Dharma becomes too secularized it is no longer worthwhile, but if it becomes too otherworldly it is difficult for people to accept it. The solution is to synthesize these two truths. It is important to remember that the Dharma is in this world, and that there is no enlightenment apart from this world. Humanistic Buddhism asserts that in the face of this modern, rapidly changing society the Dharma should modernize. The Dharma should be life-affirming, and it must offer solutions to current problems. The Dharma must remain as the essence of Buddhism, but it should function through secular learning. With the Dharma as its essence, Buddhism can relieve suffering and give us happiness, while it can use secular learning as a skillful means.

The Buddha studied India's Five Sciences extensively in his youth, and when he became a renunciant he sought instruction from many different ascetics. It was because he was so thoroughly schooled in both mundane and supramundane teachings that the Buddha was able to teach different kinds of disciples by providing the proper spiritual medicine for their particular problems.

My own studies began at Qixia Vinaya School from an early age. The library at Qixia Monastery housed many books that came from a local secular school, and it became just the right place for me during that time. Every day I would read many books, from traditional Chinese novels to works of Western literature, from essays to the works of famous authors, like *The Count of Monte Cristo*, *War and Peace*, *The Old Man and the Sea*, *Faust*, *The Sorrows of Young Werther*, *Camille*, the literature of Leo Tolstoy, the philosophy of John Dewey, and many others. I read quite a few books during that period. I also read the works of many Chinese authors, such as Hu Shi, Lin Yutang, Ba Jin, Lu Xun, Lao She, and Mao Dun.

With my busy schedule I no longer read as much as I used to, but I still like to take the time to read some books, magazines, and newspapers. I like to compare what I read to my past experiences, and see how it fits in with our daily lives. That way when I give talks I can draw upon this seemingly superficial knowledge as supporting material. While such things may not seem lofty, it is important to explain profound ideas simply, and I feel that I have never led living beings astray.

Knowledge is not unimportant, for even mundane knowledge can enhance our understanding of Buddhism. For example, I regularly encourage Buddhists to visit the various Buddhist holy sites and have led several tours myself. By visiting these sites

Buddhists can learn about the history of Buddhism, increase their faith, and focus more intently on the path. Learning about history helps us to see how things rise, fall, succeed, and fail. When we see the world we can broaden our horizons, take in a wider degree of experience, and expand our perspectives on life.

To live in this world we must be familiar with this world's body of knowledge. The more we know and understand, the better prepared we are to solve the world's problems.

During the life of the Buddha there was a monk named Sronakotivimsa who had been a music teacher before he joined the monastic order. After he ordained he was eager to attain enlightenment, so he practiced diligently day and night and never relaxed his efforts. After practicing in this way for a long time he still had not attained enlightenment, and his body and mind became exhausted. Sronakotivimsa started to think about giving up.

After the Buddha learned of this, he explained to Sronakotivimsa how spiritual cultivation is like adjusting the strings of a musical instrument: if the strings are too tight they will easily break, but if they are too loose they will not play in tune. Only by finding the middle ground between tautness and looseness is one able to play wonderful music. Spiritual cultivation is the same: being too stringent or too lax both fall short of the right path. After listening to the Buddha's instructions, Sronakotivimsa revised his method of practice, and not long afterwards he became an arhat.

Buddhism and Science

When spreading the Buddhist teachings it is not only important that we are in accord with the truth, but that we are in tune with circumstances and the spiritual capacities of living beings.

Buddhism must keep up with the times and be able to respond to modern questions.

One such question is whether or not there is life in the universe beyond our planet earth. Is there such a thing as aliens from outer space? This is a question that science would like to answer. On July 4th, 1997 NASA's Pathfinder landed on Mars, and ever since then it has seemed more possible that one day human beings would live on Mars. If humans ever live on Mars, then we will be able to answer this question and say that, yes, there are indeed Martians!

However, the *Amitabha Sutra*, composed over two thousand years ago, mentions that "one trillion Buddha lands from here, there is a realm called Ultimate Bliss, and its Buddha is named Amitabha." The sutras also mention bodhisattvas from other Buddha lands coming to hear the Buddha teach. The Buddhist sutras clearly have an idea of a wider universe that predates modern astronomy by more than two thousand years.

Buddhist truths help to validate science, and Buddhism's consistency with science shows that Buddhism is not merely a superstition. The Buddhist doctrines of the five aggregates and the four elements of earth, water, fire, and wind are a Buddhist analysis of psychology and physics. Buddhism conceives of matter as composed of atoms and time as made up of instants. The sutras mention the "three thousandfold world system," just as science has confirmed that the Milky Way is made up of countless stars. The sutras mention the Buddha "looked into a bowl of water and saw eighty-four thousand beings," just as science has confirmed the existence of microscopic life.

The Buddha would also frequently describe natural phenomena in his teachings. For example, the Buddha used five analogies to describe how the five aggregates are not real: "Form is like a patch of foam, feeling is like a water bubble, perception is like the sun's refraction,[17] mental formation is like a plantain trunk, and consciousness is like an illusion." Additionally, the *Amitabha Sutra* describes the Pure Land of Ultimate Bliss as being separated from this world by "one trillion Buddha lands" to describe a truly immense distance, and yet a single thought can take you there in the same instant it takes to form the thought.

Buddhism will interpret scientific discoveries in terms of the Buddhist teachings as science continues to develop. This can be a way for Buddhism to help to point out a possible future for science, and can lead us to think about future questions.

For example, science has helped us land a man on the moon, but can it bring us to the Pure Land of Ultimate Bliss? Science can help us land on the moon, as the moon is part of the material world. But the Pure Land is part of the spiritual world, and as such we can go there instantly.

With modern science we can replace our internal organs through transplants, but can the brain be transplanted? Can we transplant our thoughts? The Buddhist teachings say that the body is made up of the five aggregates and the four elements of earth, water, fire, and wind. But this physical body does not really exist, for it is subject to birth, aging, sickness, and death, but our true life cannot die. Thus, while it is possible to transplant organs, we will never be able to transplant life.

Medical science has even developed genetic therapy that is capable of changing our genes, but will this allow us to avoid misfortune? Actually, genetics is very similar to the Buddhist concept of karma. Karma is created through our own conduct, and each person's destiny is determined by his or her own wholesome or unwholesome karma. By doing good deeds we can naturally prevent misfortune. In a way, by doing what is wholesome and staying away from what is unwholesome we can rebuild our genetics.

Buddhism and Psychology

Humanistic Buddhism holds that we must bring together the ancient and modern, so that secular knowledge and the Buddhist teachings can complement each other. In addition to opening new avenues of thought for science, the Buddhist teachings also have many ideas to contribute to psychology. Modern psychology takes our mental life as its object of study and draws insight from medical science, philosophy, religious studies, education, sociology, and other such fields.

Psychology has been applied to various branches of learning and many different professions. Today psychology has a role in education, industry, commerce, medicine, military affairs, law, politics, society, science, art, and athletics. Psychology is steadily becoming more and more important.

Psychology observes our minds, our behavior, and our various forms of consciousness. While Western psychology studies the latent factors that develop behavior and personality, it is unable to reform human personality because of its limited scope. On the other hand, Buddhism not only possesses a complete understanding of the human mind, but it also has methods to remedy our problems. For example, the *Avatamsaka Sutra* states:

> *Understand that the three realms exist due to the mind,*
> *The same is true for the Twelve Links of Dependent Origination;*
> *Birth and death has been fabricated by the mind;*

If the mind is extinguished, birth and death come
to an end.

Buddhism analyzes and explains the mind on many levels, and uses many analogies to describe it. But most importantly, Buddhism then instructs us in how to reclaim, pacify, and purify the mind. In this way, Buddhist psychology surpasses Western psychology.

Learning Buddhist Knowledge

Buddhism is the science of philosophy, and it guides and instructs us in a way that is both rational and wisdom-oriented. Though learning and obtaining worldly knowledge can expand our horizons, Buddhism holds that if the right understanding is lacking then such knowledge can lead us in unwholesome and foolish directions. Not only will this harm the individual, but more seriously, it can be a real disaster for humanity. This is why Buddhism believes that truth is the highest form of guidance.

To develop this right understanding we should learn widely and develop extensive knowledge, but we must do so in the proper way. While we should not be too concerned about gains and losses or successes and failures, it is important to clearly distinguish between right and wrong. When we listen we should listen attentively and mindfully, and think about what is good and true in what we hear. It is also helpful to develop a close relationship with a temple or Dharma center that you feel connected to, and listen to the teachers there who are good at explaining the Dharma.

We should frequently request that the Dharma be taught and be there to listen to these teachings. Many Buddhists also find it helpful to become familiar with the *Tripitaka*, the Buddhist canon, and the works of the great Buddhist sages. When we have received the teachings we should not just move on to the next thing, but carefully consider them and reflect upon them. When we hear something that we know is good, we should let ourselves be drawn to it, and put what we know is good into practice.

Once we have begun to practice we must remember to cultivate both wisdom and merit, for our practice is incomplete unless both are present. The sutras say, "To cultivate merit without developing wisdom is like an elephant wearing a jeweled necklace. To develop wisdom without cultivating merit is like an arhat who rarely receives offerings."

As we practice we will develop wisdom, and it is important that we grasp this wisdom correctly. When we do not fully understand Buddhism, things like the doctrine of emptiness may seem scary. However, when we develop wisdom we know that emptiness does not mean nothingness, but that it is because of emptiness that all of existence is made possible. Instead of making us feel fatalistic, the Buddhist teachings on karma and cause and effect should make us feel optimistic and open-minded.

When we come to such an understanding we should share the teachings with others. We should spread the teachings far and wide and always explain them with kind and loving words.

The phrase "I have Dharma joy, and take no joy in worldly pleasures," appears many times in the sutras. Here, "Dharma" means truth, for the happiness that comes from the truth is the only truly lasting happiness. Dharma joy is found in the five precepts, the ten wholesome actions, the six perfections, and the four means of embracing. Dharma joy is found in karma, cause and effect, and the Middle Way between existence and emptiness. With Dharma joy we do not reject or become attached to the five desires or the six sense objects. We do not feel like or dislike for the worldly things in life, but instead find peace and freedom wherever we go. With Dharma joy, this present moment becomes the Pure Land of Ultimate Bliss. Dharma joy is like a ferryboat that carries us across *samsara* to the other shore that is permanent, blissful, pure, and is the true self.

Chapter Eleven

Wise Ways

The Manifestations of Wisdom

Wise Conduct

T HE *Treatise on the Awakening of Faith in Mahayana* [*Dasheng Qixin Lun*] says that living beings have "one mind that opens with two doors." One of these is the "door of suchness," which is seeing things the way they really are, and the other is the "door of *samsara*," which is seeing things the way they appear to be with our limited wisdom. Prajna wisdom is what opens the door of suchness.

Prajna is not mysterious or abstruse, but manifests itself in many ways, including how we conduct ourselves. When the Buddha simply held forth a flower and Mahakasyapa responded with a smile this began the mind-to-mind transmission from master to disciple, and Chan became a light for the world. When the Buddha became enlightened and returned to teach, the five ascetics who formerly practiced with him agreed to ignore his arrival but the Buddha's awe-inspiring conduct led them to rejoin him and pay homage to him as the Buddha. Such conduct can liberate living beings, and is a manifestation of humanistic wisdom.

The manifestation of humanistic wisdom can be seen in the daily actions of practitioners in Chan temples. Planting pine trees, hoeing the fields, sifting the rice, and sweeping the ground are all Chan. Even drinking tea, eating food, wearing robes, carrying the alms bowl, engaging in communal labor, making social calls, arching the eyebrows, and winking the eyes are Chan. Speaking, silence, movement, and stillness are all imbued with the profound meaning of Chan and contain within them the causes and conditions for attaining enlightenment.

Buddhist monastics have many rules of conduct which instill in them a high level of dignity and decorum. Sariputra, one of the Buddha's great disciples, was liberated upon seeing the dignified decorum of the monk Asvajit. Projecting a good image is not only part of being a decent person, but it can also be a method of practice.

A traditional Chan temple places a great deal of emphasis on its system of monastic rules. These rules are put in place to encourage dignified conduct and decorum and apply all aspects of how Chan practitioners are supposed to walk, stand, sit, and lie down. These rules were binding on all in the monastic community, not unlike a lease agreement you might sign to live in an apartment building. The monastic rules serve as the standard for everyday practice and organize how the monastic community conducts its business. These rules help maintain a healthy monastic community.

Chan Master Baizhang's *Rules of Purity for a Chan Temple* was also essential to the development of the traditional Chan temple. His rules organized and systematized the roles in a Chan temple by designating forty-eight separate temple officers, as well as stipulating various rules of conduct designed to encourage dignity and decorum so that the mind is not distracted and the body commits no wrongdoing. Most importantly, Baizhang's rules created the position of the abbot, who led the monastic community in cultivation and supervised the temple's affairs.

In Buddhism proper conduct means acting appropriately and maintaining serene composure when speaking or keeping silent. When we have a great level of decorum, then our conduct itself becomes a method to teach living beings.

During the Tang dynasty, the famous scholar Han Yu was exiled to Chaozhou after he submitted a report to the emperor criticizing Buddhism. Later, Han Yu went to visit Chan Master Dadian, who was meditating at the time of Han Yu's visit. Time passed, Han Yu waited, and the Chan master had still not emerged from his meditative state. The Chan master's attendant started to worry as he saw Han Yu was growing impatient, so he whispered

A Few Words of Wisdom

I do a lot of traveling, and when I visit places my schedule is usually very tight. Nonetheless, sometimes people will ask me for a few words of advice, and I do the best I can to fulfill their wishes. In Buddhism, sometimes a few words are all that it takes to unlock someone's wisdom. I hope that a few of these words will be of benefit to you:
- Remember, "I am a Buddha."
- Act willingly and happily.
- Being busy is good for you.
- Getting angry never solves the problem.
- Where there's Dharma, there's a way.
- Be the volunteer's volunteer.
- The only valuable thing is to be useful to others.

in his master's ear, "First move with concentration, then eradicate with wisdom."

What the attendant meant was that Chan Master Dadian's state of meditative concentration had touched Han Yu's heart, and that the Chan master should use his wisdom to teach him the Dharma. Han Yu heard what the attendant had whispered and was amazed to have heard such a deep teaching from an attendant, then said "I'm glad I heard such a message from an attendant!"

Humanistic Buddhist wisdom can apply anything as a skillful means, as long as it accords with the truth and takes into account current conditions. Though I may lack the all-pervasive wisdom of the ancient sages, from an early age I was fortunate to have studied at Jianshan, Qixia, and Mt. Baohua temples and even Tianning Monastery in Changzhou, receiving a complete Chan education. I had the chance to learn from many great practitioners the kind of dignity and decorum a monastic should possess. Under the tutelage of my preceptors Venerable Ruoshun and Venerable Zhuochen, as well as my Dharma teachers Venerable Renshan, Venerable Rongzhai, and Venerable Zhifeng I was ingrained with a sense of proper conduct, such that even today I have the habit of walking with my back straight and my eyes forward and only occupying half a seat when sitting. These rules have been integrated into my mental and physical life, such that even when I leave the monastery and enter the secular world I carry my Buddhist decorum with me.

I have never stopped trying to find new ways to bring aspects of the monastery into the secular world and develop new ways of teaching the Dharma. In Taiwan I have had the opportunity to organize Buddhist choirs, record Buddhist records, set up weekend schools for children, establish student groups and

Dharma lecturing teams, make Buddhist radio and TV programs, and even conduct the first ever parade with floats for the Buddha's birthday.

At Fo Guang Shan, my monastery in Taiwan, I built a "Pure Land Cave," which uses dioramas to depict the Pure Land of Ultimate Bliss as described in the *Amitabha Sutra*. Fo Guang Shan also has a Buddhist Cultural Museum to try to unite Buddhism with art and literature. The museum has been successful at publicizing the beauty of Buddhist art, while at the same time encouraging many in literary and artistic circles to develop a closer relationship with Buddhism.

The Role of the Temple

Today there are many ways to teach Buddhism such that learning the Dharma is no longer limited to Buddhist monasteries and temples. That being said, the temple will forever be the symbol of Buddhism. The temple is where the monastic community resides, where the Dharma is taught, and where the Buddha statues are enshrined. Without Buddhist temples there would be no Triple Gem of Buddha, Dharma, and Sangha, and no Buddhism. Without Buddhist temples there would be no way to disseminate the teachings and no ability to ensure that the true Dharma will last a long time.

Buddhist temples are the representatives of Buddhism; they are the center of faith and the place where devotees entrust their spirit. The buildings at the temple are there to be used to propagate the Dharma and supply what is needed to liberate living beings. The magnificent halls, quiet atmosphere, harmonious chanting, and compassionate teachings found at Buddhist temples provide people with a way to re-energize themselves regardless of how they wish to practice, even if they only wish to look up and bow to the Buddha.

If someone has a few hours free from their busy schedule and are suffering setbacks or feeling helpless and indecisive, they will go to a Buddhist temple. Buddhist temples are like refueling stations for your life, department stores for the spirit, and schools for those who seek sagehood. They are a place for good friends to meet, and a refreshing spot to rid oneself of affliction.

At Fo Guang Shan and its branch temples around the world I have tried to make sure that Buddhist temples are able to provide modern people with what they need. For this reason, Fo Guang Shan branches have lecture halls, conference rooms, sutra copying halls, lounge areas, libraries, multimedia centers, exhibition halls for cultural artifacts, art galleries, teahouses, gift

More Words of Wisdom

- You are your own best benefactor.
- Always think: what can I do for others?
- Make your words like sunlight, flowers, and pure water.
- It is better to lose everything than lose compassion.
- The bigger your heart, the bigger your accomplishment.
- People do not die, *samsara* merely shifts.
- You must understand truth, and not simply talk about it. Only by understanding the truth can you naturally and happily do good.
- Give people confidence; give people joy; give people hope; and give people ease.
- It is easy to manage your wealth, manage your affairs, and manage people. It is hard to manage the mind.
- Learning Buddhism is not about suffering, but the condition of suffering helps us progress.

shops, parking garages, and even research rooms and computer labs.

To accommodate the needs of modern office workers there are even Fo Guang Shan branches in urban areas, as well as *Beautiful Life TV*, a Buddhist satellite television station, and online distance learning courses in Buddhist studies. The traditional time for morning chanting is pushed back to accommodate the schedules of modern people, and major Dharma services are always conducted during daylight hours.

The Dharma is like a lighthouse that can guide us through life and spare us from becoming lost in the vast and open sea. Prajna is like a light that illuminates the darkened room of our ignorance and brings together the distinctions between ourselves and others. With prajna, our minds are not affected by like or dislike for external circumstances, and we can turn our attachments into compassion for living beings.

The *Sutra on the Eight Realizations of a Bodhisattva* [*Ba Daren Jue Jing*] says, "Always remember to remain content; find happiness in poverty and devotion to the path. The pursuit of wisdom is the only worthy endeavor." Prajna purifies our thoughts and elevates our morality. It is through prajna wisdom that we see that pleasure and pain share the same essence, purity and defilement become one, and poverty and wealth can both be enjoyed freely. Prajna allows us to subdue our minds and generate the aspiration to liberate all living beings through our compassion. This is prajna at its highest level.

Chapter Twelve

One World
The Perfection of Wisdom

Oneness and Coexistence

H UMAN BEINGS ARE social animals. We cannot live on our own: when we are at home we rely on our parents, and when we go out we rely on our friends. We are connected to all kinds of people from all levels of society, many of whom we do not even know. We need workers to make fabric so we can wear clothes and we need farmers to plant crops so we can eat food. Every road we walk on was built by someone else, and each brick and tile in our home was built by another person. The mountains, lakes, streams, and other scenic spots that we enjoy are all maintained by others. There are many, many more ways that we need to rely on others to make our lives possible. If we were to leave society and all its people there would simply be no way to survive.

All phenomena in the universe mutually bring about and complete each other, while all living beings have a relationship of oneness and coexistence. The world can only enjoy peace and happiness when everyone understands the importance of oneness and coexistence. Only those who understand oneness and coexistence are truly wise, for without this relationship humanistic wisdom can never be perfected.

Oneness means equality and tolerance. For example, the human body has eyes, ears, a nose, a tongue, hands, and feet, and yet these different organs are all a part of the same body. The earth is made up of different countries, ethnicities, and regions, yet we all live together and share a dependence on the earth. Human beings may be male or female, young or old, strong or weak, and wise or foolish, yet we are all living things born because of a combination of many conditions. Human beings may vary in a million different ways, but the purity of their Buddha nature allows them to be one.

Coexistence means compassion and harmony. All living beings depend upon one another. The Buddhist sutras contain a parable about how a person who could not see, a person who could not walk, and a person who could not speak escaped from a burning building by relying on each other for guidance, support, and help. In the same way, a brilliant play does not only depend on the great performance of the main actors, but requires the seamless coordination of the supporting roles. We need each individual to contribute the strength of his or her trade or profession in order to establish a peaceful and harmonious society.

The earth that we live on is part of a large universe, while each of our bodies is like a small universe. This smaller universe and the larger universe are actually vitally connected. If we say a few words, electricity can transmit them around the world. A puff of air that we exhale can create a windstorm in the sky above. We should never think of ourselves as only individuals.

The earth is so big and space is so vast, how much of it can we possibly care about? Do you remember the bird flu that frightened the whole world? That whole epidemic was caused simply because a single small animal caught a cold. Since the human body did not have any immunity against it, people became infected and even died from the disease. This example shows us that the world has no national boundaries, and that everyone is related through oneness and coexistence.

Many trees must grow together before they can become a forest. When we visit the mountains we can see many trees thriving several thousand feet above sea level. These trees will not stop growing because of you or me, for they have grown together by relying on one another and sharing in their prosperity. The rivers, streams, and lakes join the ocean a little at a time, and the ocean becomes great by containing them all. A single lamp may be lit, and then more and more lamps can be lit, one by one, from that single light, until each lamp shines on all others, just as each Buddha has followed previous Buddhas on the same path, like a series of never ending lights. This is oneness and coexistence.

Birds fly together with their mates, fish swim together with their companions, and male and female phoenixes soar through the sky in pairs. These creatures naturally unite in harmony, which is why people admire them so. Even a lion can live together with a dog, and dogs and cats can depend on each other to live. There are no natural enemies in this world; it only appears this way sometimes because of each animal's uniquely acquired traits. Some naturally enjoy living high in the mountains, while others habitually live near ground level. Some dwell in mountain caves, while others hide away deep in the sea. There is no limit to where and how life can occur, for even in the heat of the desert a cactus proudly blooms with flowers of various colors. All forms of life can coexist and survive together in nature.

Action in a United World

The Buddha stressed that everything in the world is formed from the four elements of earth, water, fire, and wind and is a combination of the five aggregates. Because of this, we can say that I am part of you, and you are part of me. It is this spirit of harmony which is most emphasized in Humanistic Buddhism. The Buddha always stressed the importance of service, respect, generosity, and joyful giving no matter which country or region he happened to be in so that everyone would come to understand respect and harmonious coexistence.

Consider the beautiful lands of ancient China, Japan, and Korea: which one of these did not benefit from the development of Buddhism? Today Humanistic Buddhism advocates mutual contact and communication as a way of achieving unity of faith. Even if differences remain we can still respect one another. We encourage friendship through disaster relief and assistance; we encourage communication by using various written and spoken languages; and we build bridges between various cultures by convening academic conferences. It is in this way that we strengthen the cause of mutual understanding and tolerance.

This world is home to us all and we can all help each other by coming together and providing relief. Fo Guang Shan has set aside plots of land on Australia's Gold Coast, the Hawaiian islands, and in Deer Park, New York, to prepare to provide services for the elderly and preschool education. Our main goal is to ensure that we respect the old and protect the young. To these ends we provide medical care for older folks suffering financial difficulties, and have set up scholarships, Boy Scouts and Girl Scouts troops, and kindergartens for young people.

The Buddha's Light International Association has also participated in charitable programs for many years throughout the world. In countries with poorer living standards, the BLIA assists the local people by building houses, supplying food, providing medical care, and offering education. For countries with a mature social welfare system, the BLIA undertakes activities like charity bazaars, free clinics, and blood drives, as well as providing institutional care and comfort for the disadvantaged who are entering old folks' homes, orphanages, reformatories, and special education institutes.

Towards the Future

The true meaning of equality is that there is no difference between the one and the many. Most people wish they had more and dislike having less, and this creates a lot of confusion and unwholesome karma through comparing things and making calculations. This is also why the world is embroiled in such endless turmoil. From a Buddhist perspective, one is actually the many, and the many are one. Since all phenomena coexist in oneness every single thing has an unbreakable connection to the whole. The world can only have peace when there is equality, and there can only be equality when the great respect the small, when those who have more respect those who have less, and when the strong respect the weak.

Bodhisattvas realize that prajna is the mother of all Buddhas, that all phenomena arise and cease due to causes and conditions, that the Three Dharma Seals are the truth of the universe, that the four elements do not exist independently of one another, that the five aggregates are empty, and that all things exist in a relationship of oneness and coexistence. By realizing these truths bodhisattvas come to understand the Law of Dependent Origination and the unity of emptiness and existence, and apply these supramundane teachings to undertake mundane matters.

Sometimes people wonder if there is such a thing as destiny, when in fact our destiny comes from our causes and conditions. The positive and negative results of our karma determine our destiny. To live in the world we must create good connections with others so that we can have a bright future. When other people create good causes and conditions for us, we should do what we can to create good causes and conditions for them. Serving as causes and conditions for one another is oneness and coexistence.

Oneness and coexistence are broad and profound. Not only is everything we require to live drawn from the fruits of society's hard labor, but there even exists a relationship of oneness and coexistence between human beings and nature as well. These days serious natural disasters like earthquakes, tsunamis, and typhoons occur frequently throughout the world. These seem like natural calamities, but in fact they are the result of nature's backlash against humanity's destruction of the environment. For example, the tropical rainforests in South America can seriously impact the survival of the whole human race because they regulate the air and temperature of the entire globe. The United Nations has provided financial subsidies with the hope that they will end deforestation and protect the rainforests, but the fact of the matter is that the rainforests continue to slowly disappear. One of the indirect causes of the hundreds of deaths in New Orleans due to Hurricane Katrina was the overdevelopment of the wetlands.

The greatest danger humanity faces today is its long-standing tendency to consider all phenomena solely from its own perspective. We use what can be used and eliminate anything that runs contrary to this purpose. This has resulted in a steady march towards self-destruction. Humanity is destroying its own future.

Buddhism speaks of "oneness and coexistence" because our mutual survival is made possible through mutual coexistence. When the Buddhist teaching of generosity is considered on a macro level it becomes the oneness of the self and others. Our property can be shared with others, and our wisdom need not be kept private. Everything I have need not be enjoyed by me alone; instead I can give something back to people who need it.

Many of the Buddhist teachings take on new significance when viewed in terms of oneness and coexistence. Buddhism teaches us to cherish our blessings because it is only by cherishing our natural resources that human beings can live in peace on earth. The Buddhist teaching on cause and effect shows the interdependence of all living beings, and the Buddhist attitude of unconditional loving kindness and compassion is the basis of advancing public welfare.

Nations and societies are composed of various causal relationships and are established through the joint efforts of their peoples. With this understanding we should throw away the ideas of "survival of the fittest" and instead adopt a perspective of equality and mutual benefit. Anything that benefits living beings, from great endeavors like the peace movement and the environmental movement to smaller undertakings like building bridges and roads, offering someone a lamp or some tea, or giving encouragement should be undertaken with everyone's best effort whenever possible. We must unite our effort to accomplish great things.

When we look at the world as a whole we can see that only these Buddhist truths can protect the environment and save us from a world in danger. Only when equality is given to all living beings will we eliminate our attachment to the self. The compassionate protection of life is the only thing that will reduce humanity's penchant for killing. Only by understanding principles from the facts will we be able to open up our blocked spirit.

The *Diamond Sutra* says, "The Dharma is equal, for there is no high or low." Because of the great wisdom of the equality of nature and emptiness, the equality of phenomena and principle, and the equality of ordinary beings and Buddhas, the mind can encompass the vastness of space and contain as many worlds as there are grains of sand in the Ganges River. As the Buddha said in the *Lankavatara Sutra,* "All sentient beings are just like me." We can realize unconditional loving kindness and compassion when we understand oneness and coexistence.

To Serve the World

Because human beings are such social animals, the Buddha taught his disciples to have good manners so they could join a group and live together. He taught his disciples to be modest and polite, know their proper place, listen deeply, and to receive instructions with conviction and conscientiously put them into practice. This was a long, long time ago, and yet one still cannot help but be struck by such kindness and sense of purpose today.

Even though we could never live apart from each other, wars still continue around the world without end. Wars are about killing people, but if we could ever actually kill all the other people and only one of us was left, that person would find it impossible to survive. Hurting other people actually hurts us, just as benefiting others benefits us. Everyone is related to one another through causes and conditions.

In Buddhism there are many stories about Yama, the Lord of Death. Yama is said to reside in hell and pass judgment on those who have died. One day there was a procession of ghosts before him, waiting to be judged. Yama said to the first ghost, "In life you committed murder and robbery. You broke the law and went against the standards of society. I will now sentence you to suffer in hell for one hundred years, after which you will be reborn as a human being."

Another ghost stepped before him, and this time Yama said, "In life you only cared about drinking, eating, and enjoying yourself. You became rich through deceit or by force. You did not respect or obey your parents, nor did you do anything to benefit society. I will now sentence you to suffer in hell for fifty years, after which you will be reborn as a human being."

The next ghost had been a news reporter during his life, and Yama said to him, "You are sentenced to Avici hell,[18] where you will be tormented without reprieve."

Once he heard his sentence the former reporter protested, "Those other two committed all kinds of wrongdoing, and you only sentenced them to fifty and one hundred years! I was a mere news reporter who did not rob or kill anyone. Why should I be sentenced to Avici hell?"

The Lord of Death replied, "The articles you wrote laid ruin to the human heart. Even today your writings still circulate around the world and bring harm to others. As for the other two, their acts were harmful only once and that was it. Not until the poisonous influence of the words you have written has completely disappeared will you even have an opportunity to seek a reprieve!"

We should not think that when we harm others we are free from any responsibility. Each individual is related to the larger society through causes and conditions. Thus, it is only through coexistence that any of us can have an auspicious life. All life, irrespective of its species or form, whether it swims in the water, flies in the sky, or crawls on the earth, exists in common as one entity through coexistence.

As the Buddha said in the *Diamond Sutra,* "All sentient beings, whether they are born from eggs, born from a womb, born in moisture, or born from transformation; whether they are with form or without form; whether they are with perception, without perception, or are neither with perception nor without perception; I will cause them all to enter *nirvana* without remainder, liberating them." We must look upon all living beings as if they were one of our six sense organs, for we cannot do without a single one. If we can see all life like this, then everyone will be a compassionate person of oneness and coexistence.

As religious people our purpose should be to rid ourselves of selfishness and foster a civic spirit. Selfishness only compresses our spirit and gives us a shallow vision of the world. Instead, we should expand ourselves and widen our vision. This is a world of oneness and coexistence, wherein each living thing is dependent upon all the others for its very existence. This communal existence means communal prosperity. Regardless of how the brightness of the sun, the moon, and the stars in the sky compare to one another, each adds to the others' splendor. The mountains, hills, and canyons of the earth may be high or low, but together they form the undulating continuity of this planet. Each form of life in the universe, no matter how marvelous or rare, complements and completes each other no matter how similar or different they may be.

The universe is originally a realm of perfect oneness and coexistence. Everyone in it should have compassion, cherish the larger family of the universe, and treat all living beings equally. When we realize that we all live in the same community we can let go of our one-sided sense of self and look out for each other. When we know that we are all one, we can see that all living beings are equal, and respect all beings' right to life. When we see how we can all coexist we will develop loving kindness, compassion, joy, and equanimity for all. This is the only way to make this world into a humanistic Pure Land of peace and joy. This goal can only be realized when every person fully attains prajna.

The Threefold Training

We, as Buddhists, cannot do without morality, meditative concentration, and wisdom. Thousands of Buddhist sutras speak of this "threefold training" at every turn, and generations of Buddhist masters have promoted this practice.

The *Connected Discourses of the Buddha* says, "Those who have fully completed the threefold training show the correct action of a monastic." The *Great Universal Collection Sutra* says, "What are known as morality, meditative concentration, and wisdom constitute the unsurpassed *dharani*[19] that can purify the three karmas, and are what all people love." The *Sutra on the Questions of Haihui Bodhisattva on the Practice of the Pure Seals* says, "Those who hold and protect the true Dharma of all the Buddhas have purified all the karma of body, speech, and mind; and the purity of their morality, meditative concentration, and wisdom is also the same. They attain the wisdom of liberation and the purity of goodness."

The fourth century Buddhist master Daoan said, "The world-honored one established the teachings in three parts: the first of these was the precepts, the second was meditative concentration, and the third was wisdom. The three of these represent the entrance to the path and the key to *nirvana*. The precepts are like a brave general that cuts off the three poisons, meditative concentration is like a sharp weapon that ends distraction, and wisdom is like a miracle doctor who applies medicine to relieve sickness."

Kumarajiva, the famous fourth century monastic who translated many Buddhist sutras into Chinese, once said, "Holding to the precepts is being able to subjugate affliction and lessen its power. Meditative concentration is being able to block affliction like a mountain of rocks cutting off a river. Wisdom is being able to destroy affliction so that absolutely nothing is left."

The threefold training, the combination of developing morality, meditative concentration, and wisdom is uniquely suited for humanity. The sutras say that human beings have three characteristics that are not shared by any other beings in the six realms of existence: the pursuit of purity, patient diligence, and the accumulation of wisdom. Our pursuit of morality, meditative concentration, and wisdom are linked to these three unique characteristics, and give us the best access to the Way.

The threefold practice is specially suited to eliminate greed, anger, and delusion. By observing the precepts we foster good habits like hard work, thrift, joyful giving, and compassion which can counteract greed. Meditative concentration can purify our thinking so that when we encounter adversity we will not have thoughts of anger. Applying prajna allows us to transform our delusion into enlightenment.

The threefold training is a good way to approach the vast expanse of the Buddhist teachings. For example, the threefold practice is also another way to approach the practice of the Noble

ॉ

Eightfold Path. The training of morality is the same as cultivating right speech, right action, and right livelihood. The training of meditative concentration is the same as cultivating right mindfulness and right meditative concentration. The training of wisdom is the same as cultivating right view and right thought. The last part of the Noble Eightfold path, right effort, encompasses all of the threefold training

The threefold training is also a way to pursue the six perfections. The first four perfections, giving, morality, patience, and diligence are all part of training our morality. The last two perfections, the perfection of meditative concentration and the perfection of prajna, correspond directly to the training of meditative concentration and the training of wisdom.

The threefold training focuses equally on cultivating merit and wisdom, and emphasizes both practice and understanding. It is only by diligently cultivating morality, meditative concentration, and wisdom that we can eliminate greed, anger, and delusion, and secure perfect blessings for our life.

Notes

1. *Dharma* is a Sanskrit word meaning "truth" or "reality." It is also the collective name for the Buddha's teachings.
2. A *Siksamana* is a woman who observes six precepts, often as preparation for full ordination as a Buddhist nun.
3. *Tathagata* is another name for the Buddha, and was the Buddha's preferred way of referring to himself. It means "Thus come" and "Thus gone."
4. A sravaka is a Buddhist practitioner who has been liberated from the cycle of rebirth after listening to the Buddha's teachings, but does not seek to become a Buddha.
5. A bodhisattva is a being who has vowed to become a Buddha by liberating himself and all living beings.
6. Dharma guardians are celestial beings who protect Buddhism.
7. An arhat is a type of Buddhist sage who has escaped the cycle of rebirth.
8. *Samadhi* is a Sanskrit word that denotes a state of deep concentration where one is completely focused.
9. *Kalpa* is a Sanskrit word meaning an incalculably long period of time.
10. The supreme marks are a set of physical characteristics acquired from past good karma. Possessing all supreme marks identifies one as a Buddha or a great king.

11. In this instance *dharma* means "phenomena," and is the sense object associated with the mind. To distinguish this use of the word from others, when "dharma" is used to denote "phenomena" all lowercase letters are used.

12. The dharma realm is the true nature of the world we live in, and is where all phenomena arise, abide, and cease.

13. An asura is a type of celestial being which is consumed with anger and jealousy.

14. Mara is a celestial being who rules over desire and is an opponent of the Buddha. Mara tries to prevent practitioners from attaining enlightenment.

15. A pratyekabuddha is a practitioner who attains enlightenment on his own, rather than by hearing the teachings of a Buddha.

16. A Pure Land is a realm created by a Buddha's vows that is free of suffering and impurity. Those reborn in a Pure Land can practice Buddhism more easily.

17. "The sun's refraction" refers to the phenomena where the sun shines on an area of open land and it looks like a sheet of water.

18. There are many different hells in Buddhist cosmology. Avici hell is the worst of the hell realms, and beings who are reborn there suffer for incalculably long periods of time.

19. A *dharani* is a Buddhist mantra that has various special powers when recited.

Appendix 1

The Twenty Greatest Things in Life

The Twenty Greatest Things in Life was composed by Venerable Master Hsing Yun as a compliment to the Buddhist precepts. For years he has used this list in his teaching, and it is provided here for reference.

The Twenty Greatest Things in Life

1. The greatest enemy in life is the self.
2. The greatest defect in life is selfishness.
3. The greatest sadness in life is ignorance.
4. The greatest mistake in life is to hold wrong views.
5. The greatest failure in life is arrogance.
6. The greatest affliction in life is desire.
7. The greatest ignorance in life is resentment.
8. The greatest worry in life is life and death.
9. The greatest error in life is transgression.
10. The greatest confusion in life is in arguing over right and wrong.

11. The greatest virtue in life is compassion.

12. The greatest courage in life is in acknowledging your mistakes.

13. The greatest gain in life is contentment.

14. The greatest source of power in life is faith.

15. The greatest possession in life is gratitude.

16. The greatest cultivation in life is the cultivation of tolerance.

17. The greatest resource in life is dignity.

18. The greatest happiness in life is Dharma joy.

19. The greatest hope in life is peace.

20. The greatest vow in life is the vow to benefit living beings.

Appendix 2

Humanistic Buddhism's Modern Rules of Conduct

Ten Rules for Society

1. While laypeople may participate in politics, monastics should limit themselves to discussing politics. Monastics should never be involved in actual governance.
2. When engaging in politics do not abuse your power.
3. When engaging in politics work only for the public good. Accept and decline political office as conditions dictate.
4. When holding political office, make serving the people your first priority.
5. Do not betray your country, engage in spying, or divulge national secrets.
6. Maintain right livelihood by not working in an illegal or harmful profession.
7. Have professional ethics and act within the law.
8. In business treat everyone honestly and only profit from your own work.

9. Do not engage in extortion, fraud, counterfeiting, deception, misrepresentation, prostitution, or in spreading internet viruses.
10. Be trustworthy and live harmoniously.

Ten Rules for Home Life

1. Maintain a happy family life. Those who are older should be compassionate and those who are younger should be obedient.
2. Take the initiative in doing household chores, and keep everything neat and tidy.
3. Live simply and be frugal.
4. Respect every member of the family as an individual, and cherish in particular elders, women, and children.
5. Maintain a home life that adds to life's pleasures and elevates your spirit. Be kind to the community in which you live, and look after seniors who live alone.
6. Speak softly so as not to disturb your neighbors.
7. Spend free time with your family rather than engage in unnecessary social engagements. When going out, inform your family when you go and tell them when you will return so they will not worry.
8. Tidy up a room after you are no longer using it to make it ready for the next person.
9. Observe good home safety practices to protect your family from harm.
10. Spend money wisely and make a budget. Be careful when borrowing or lending money, even to close friends.

Ten Rules for Relationships

1. Build a good reputation, and be someone others can rely on.
2. Respect other people's privacy.
3. Do not abuse or exploit your workers.
4. Respect your workplace, be optimistic, and strive to improve yourself. Do not base your business decisions on emotions or say "no" too easily.
5. Maintain professional ethics. Do not waste public or company property, maintain the company's confidentiality, do not blame others, and do not vent your dissatisfactions.
6. Keep your desk clean and care for the office.
7. When answering business calls speak softly, and be brief and to the point. Do not use the office phones or computers for personal use.
8. Do not become angry if you feel you have been wronged at work. Do not put off the things that should be done, nor ignore the instructions of your superiors. Take the initiative in making reports and do not conceal anything.
9. Care for and listen to your subordinates, and share with them any honor or reward.
10. Work together with others with mutual respect and observe a division of labor.

Ten Rules for Living

1. Develop the habit of reading books.
2. Get rid of distractions and break your bad habits.
3. Maintain a balance between rest and work, and keep a regular schedule.
4. Monastics should get up before six o'clock in the morning and laypeople should get up no later than seven o'clock.

5. Unless there is some special occasion, do not chat on the phone after ten o'clock. Pay attention to time differences when making long distance calls.
6. When visiting friends, make an appointment, arrive on time, and do not stay too long.
7. Have a dignified demeanor. Do not appear unkempt or untidy.
8. Speak simply and to the point, and use refined and polite diction. Do not spout worthless chatter, sow discord, use harsh language, or damage another's faith.
9. When driving, follow the rules of the road.
10. When traveling abroad be respectful of local customs and try to absorb the best the local culture has to offer.

Ten Rules for the Environment

1. Do not recklessly dig holes or cut down trees. Don't build in violation of building codes.
2. Do not abandon your pets or inappropriately free animals.
3. Do not abuse animals. Do not kill and eat animals when they are nursing, and do not eat live animals.
4. Do not kill or capture animals en masse.
5. Do not wear clothing made from animal skin or fur.
6. Cherish trees, plants, and flowers, and do not pick them as you please. Instead, plant trees.
7. Sort through your garbage and do not throw things away indiscriminately.
8. Consume water, electricity, food, and clothing sparingly.
9. Cherish your blessings, for this is like applying environmental protection to yourself.
10. Remove defilement from the mind, and remove pollution from the environment.

Ten Rules for International Relations

1. A nation's people should be in harmony. Do not engage in any divisive behavior.
2. There should be equality among all races. Do not engage in any behavior that creates opposition or disrespect.
3. Respect and protect the rights of all human beings.
4. Respect all living beings' right to life.
5. War is the most uncivilized act. War destroys lives, property, culture, and separates mothers from their children. Develop a love of peace, and live a life of oneness and coexistence with all nations.
6. Develop friendly international relations. Encourage international trade, conduct international conferences, and respect international and interracial marriage.
7. Be a citizen of the world, share your language and your culture, promote equality among all races, and cooperate economically.
8. Respect and encourage immigration and tourism. Likewise, obey local laws when traveling.
9. Supply aid and assistance during international disasters.
10. Have respect and tolerance for all religions.

Ten Rules for Education

1. Parents should care for their children's needs and be responsible for raising them. Parents should provide a good education at home and teach their children good habits.
2. Schools should impart knowledge, keep students well-informed, and refine their moral character.
3. Learn various skills and professions.
4. Never stop learning, and spend your life learning to serve, contribute, benefit others, respect yourself and others, and live in harmony.

5.   Do not gamble, visit prostitutes, take drugs, smoke cigarettes, or drink alcohol. Exercise to maintain your health, and be punctual, trustworthy, true to your faith, and law-abiding.
6.   Develop general knowledge, especially in geography and history.
7.   Maintain pure thinking and correct understanding.
8.   Learn to have a compassionate character, taking the Buddhas and bodhisattvas as models.
9.   Develop your morality through the Buddhist teachings and the teachings of other religions and philosophies.
10. Be self-aware and comprehend things. Raise doubts and delve into the meanings of things.

Ten Rules for Religion

1.   Money should never pass between laypeople and monastics, nor should any loans be made between them.
2.   Interactions between the monastic order and the lay community should be established with correct understanding. The monastic community should manage its own affairs and not support those monastics who break the precepts.
3.   BLIA members should deal with disputes according to the Seven Rules for Eliminating Conflict.
4.   Try to attend morning and evening chanting, and practice on your own once a week or perform a half-day retreat.
5.   Read from *Pearls of Wisdom* and take refuge in the Triple Gem each day.
6.   Have faith in karma and have the right view on impermanence, suffering, emptiness, and dependent origination. Practice the Noble Eightfold Path.
7.   Hold marriages, funerals, and celebrate moving to a new home with a Buddhist ceremony.

8. Plan ahead for your spiritual life, including participating in Buddhist ceremonies and retreats.

9. At parties and social gatherings, be forthright about being a Buddhist. Do not drink to excess nor urge anyone to drink. If it is awkward not to drink, substitute tea for wine.

10. Make offerings to a good temple as you please, but not so much that you feel annoyed or regretful.

Appendix 3

Life's One Hundred Tasks

This list of one hundred tasks was developed by Venerable Master Hsing Yun in 2005 as a way to guide our lives. If you already do at least ten of these activities you are on the right track. See if you can work up to accomplishing all one hundred tasks.

The Ten Tasks of Daily Life

1. Read from at least one newspaper and one good book each day.
2. Keep a good balance between rest and work. Keep set hours for going to bed and waking up in the morning. Eat the same amount of food for your three meals each day.
3. Develop an exercise routine and walk at least five thousand steps each day.
4. Stay away from tobacco, alcohol, pornography, and drugs. Govern and regulate your own life.
5. Cherish your blessings and be frugal. Do not buy things thoughtlessly or indulgently
6. Do not eat snacks foolishly nor express anger thoughtlessly.

7. Recite the Buddha's name three times at each meal, and observe the Five Contemplations when eating at home.
8. Go on a journey by yourself.
9. Give away all your possessions at least once in your lifetime to experience the state of emptiness.
10. Manage your time well, use your space well, and be in harmony with the world.

Twenty-Four Tasks to Establish Yourself

11. Use your abilities to help other people.
12. Understand karma and the Law of Cause and Effect.
13. Develop right understanding and right view. Do not simply repeat what others have said and be led blindly by others.
14. Have confidence in yourself, have expectations for yourself, and set goals for yourself.
15. During your life learn at least three different specialized skills, like piloting an airplane, cooking, or doing electrical work.
16. Learn to speak and write articulately. Learn to listen, think, laugh, sing, and paint.
17. Whatever you do, do it well.
18. Do not be greedy for the possessions of others or stingy with your own wealth.
19. Learn to be a sharp observer and consider things from all angles. Be tolerant of others and all-encompassing.
20. Frequently share your joy, compassion, glory, and success with others.
21. Do not gossip.
22. Be self-disciplined, self-realized, and self-enlightened.
23. Control your emotions and your temper and do not be manipulated by them.

24. Plan ahead and use your time wisely.
25. Reach for your goals and aim high. Look to the future instead of looking back at the past.
26. Do not ask others for help, but find help from within.
27. Change your bad habits. Create your own future instead of waiting for the right opportunity to arise.
28. Find joy and happiness in your work and then spread that joy to others.
29. Do not get angry and lose your temper, for this cannot solve your problems. Instead be calm and peaceful.
30. Prefer to be unintelligent rather than unreasonable. Prefer poverty to losing your compassion.
31. Take initiative and be fearless, but think before you act.
32. Know that there is no absolute difficulty or ease. Make what is difficult easy with diligence, and do not allow what is easy to become difficult through sloth.
33. Forget your selfish thoughts and dedicate yourself to justice, truth, fairness, and the common good.
34. Find the wisdom and strength to resist the temptations of wealth, sex, fame, and food. Do not handle official business with personal emotions, but make decisions based on morality and fairness.

Thirteen Tasks for Dealing with Others

35. Think of other people first when there is some benefit to be had, and do not betray others for your own gain.
36. Do not speak of your own merits or the faults of others.
37. Concern yourself only with what is right and wrong, not with what was gained or lost.
38. Do not violate the rights of others for your own benefit. Let other people benefit instead.

39. Do not ridicule others just to make yourself feel good. Praise others instead and earn their recognition.
40. Do not become jealous of other people's good qualities. Respect these people and rejoice in their good example.
41. Plan your career well, use your money wisely, purify your emotions, and remain unattached to fame and honor.
42. Find peace wherever you are. Live in accordance with conditions as they arise. Find freedom in every thought and joy in every act.
43. Honor and disgrace are a natural part of life. Diminish your desire for all things so that you can be happy and contented.
44. Be a kind and honest person.
45. Do not forget your initial resolve, and be willing to forgive old grudges against friends. Do what is right without being asked. Be constant and yet adaptable.
46. Train yourself to be patient and understand, accept, take responsibility for, resolve, and remove external circumstances. Develop the patience for life, the patience for phenomena, and the patience for the non-arising of phenomena.
47. Learn to endure outside pressures as if there were no pressures at all. Instead, let these pressures give you power.

Twenty Rules for Human Relations

48. Help other people. Helping others is the same as helping yourself. Being considerate towards others is the same as caring for yourself.
49. Accommodate other people who seek to do good and find a common goal.
50. Be polite, courteous, and humble. Work towards the greater good even if it gives you some trouble.

51. Be gentle and humble when dealing with others. Be kind to them in word and deed.
52. Be calm, peaceful, and harmonious with others. Be diligent and hard-working at your job.
53. Treat others with honesty so that everyone is happy. Treat guests with respect to make them feel at home.
54. When meeting other people say at least three sentences to them and accompany them for a while. Be reasonable and always put a smile on your face.
55. Be respectful, praising, and tolerant of others.
56. Speak less when you are happy and do not take your anger out on others.
57. Listen well and be able to pick out the essence of what is said.
58. Do not be brash, but learn the noble art of subtlety.
59. Reproach others with comforting words, criticize with compliments, reprimand with praises, and give orders with respect.
60. Be sincere, passionate, and polite. Say "please," "thank you," and "sorry."
61. Educate and encourage young people. Care for and look after the elderly. Assist and guide the disabled. Advise and be considerate towards the depressed.
62. Care for your neighbors and community, and participate in local events. Look out for each other and coexist in harmony.
63. Attend to and care for your parents and elders. Give young people opportunities and offer guidance whenever needed.
64. Help other people and never ask for anything in return. Do good deeds and be a volunteer for all of humanity.
65. Listen to words of kindness and do not forget them.
66. Be reasonable in all things.

67. Reflect on yourself in all situations. Do not blame others for your unhappiness, for everything is due to cause and effect.

Fifteen Rules on Sincerity

68. Do no be jealous of those who have done good deeds, spoken kind words, or are respected by others. Instead, follow their example.
69. Be thankful to the kindhearted, be grateful to those who help you, and be touched by virtuous acts.
70. Do things which touch other people's hearts, and allow yourself to be touched by the kindness of others.
71. Accept being wronged, unjust treatment, setbacks, and humiliation. Only then can you accept honor.
72. Strengthen yourself through ascetic practice.
73. Find three people who can serve as lifetime role models, then emulate them.
74. Draw yourself to good Dharma friends. If you encounter a wise teacher stay close to that teacher, be loyal, and do not disobey him.
75. Give up any unreasonable attachments and humbly accept the truth. Only by being humble can you gain something beneficial, for arrogance will surely lead to failure.
76. Discover your greatest shortcoming and be willing to correct it.
77. Admit your own mistakes.
78. Remember the mistakes you have committed in the past, constantly remind yourself of them, and do not make the same mistake again.
79. Reflect upon yourself before you blame other people. Only by fairly assessing your own merits and faults will you have the right to judge others.

80. Cherish, protect, and respect life. Never harm life.
81. Do not become blinded by love or betray yourself for money.
82. Learn to accept disadvantages, and see that disadvantages can sometimes be advantages.

Eighteen Rules for Spiritual Cultivation

83. Meditate for five minutes or read a prayer from *Pearls of Wisdom* once each day.
84. Spend at least half a day in solitude each week for self-reflection. Be a vegetarian for at least one day each month to foster compassion.
85. Each day do good deeds, speak good words, and keep good thoughts.
86. Observe the Seven Admonitions every day.
87. Have deep faith in the Dharma. Always do what is wholesome and do nothing that is unwholesome.
88. Keep your promises.
89. Feel shame for what you do not know, what you cannot do, the parts of you that are impure, and the wrongs you have done.
90. Think of what is good and beautiful instead of what is sad and sorrowful. Turn your mind into a factory that produces nothing but good.
91. Sympathize with those less fortunate than you and pray that they are blessed.
92. Give, for it brings true wealth. Let go, for it is the only way to gain anything.
93. Accumulate merit by giving according to your ability.
94. Become an organ donor.
95. Allow other people to be great, and be willing to be small. Allow other people to have things, and be willing to go without.

Allow other people to be happy, and be willing to suffer. Allow other people to be right, and be willing to be wrong.

96. Do not be suspicious or jealous of others.

97. Do not cling to gains or losses. Do not compare what you have or do not have to others.

98. Never infect others with your own sadness and do not bring your worries to bed.

99. Know how to change your mind, transform your nature, and turn around to mend your ways.

100. Ensure that your behavior and understanding are in accord with one another. Do not be enlightened in theory but ignorant in practice.

About the Author

Founder of the Fo Guang Shan (Buddha's Light Mountain) Buddhist Order and the Buddha's Light International Association, Venerable Master Hsing Yun has dedicated his life to teaching Humanistic Buddhism, which seeks to realize spiritual cultivation in everyday living.

Master Hsing Yun is the 48th Patriarch of the Linji Chan School. Born in Jiangsu Province, China in 1927, he was tonsured under Venerable Master Zhikai at the age of twelve and became a novice monk at Qixia Vinaya College. He was fully ordained in 1941 following years of strict monastic training. When he left Jiaoshan Buddhist College at the age of twenty, he had studied for almost ten years in a monastery.

Due to the civil war in China, Master Hsing Yun moved to Taiwan in 1949 where he undertook the revitalization of Chinese Mahayana Buddhism. He began fulfilling his vow to promote the Dharma by starting chanting groups, student and youth groups, and other civic-minded organizations with Leiyin Temple in Ilan as his base. Since the founding of Fo Guang Shan monastery in Kaohsiung in 1967, more than two hundred temples have been established worldwide. Hsi Lai Temple, the symbolic torch of the Dharma spreading to the West, was built in 1988 near Los Angeles.

Master Hsing Yun has been guiding Buddhism on a course of modernization by integrating Buddhist values into education, cultural activities, charity, and religious practices. To achieve these ends, he travels all over the world, giving lectures and actively engaging in religious dialogue. The Fo Guang Shan organization also oversees sixteen Buddhist colleges and four universities, one of which is the University of the West in Rosemead, California.

Other Works by Venerable Master Hsing Yun:

The Core Teachings

Traveling to the Other Shore
The Buddha's Stories on the Six Perfections

Footprints in the Ganges
The Buddha's Stories on Cultivation and Compassion

Opening the Mind's Eye
Clarity and Spaciousness in Buddhist Practice

Between Ignorance and Enlightenment

Infinite Compassion, Endless Wisdom
The Practice of the Bodhisattva Path

Where is Your Buddha Nature?
Stories to Instruct and Inspire

Being Good
Buddhist Ethics for Everyday Life

Chan Heart, Chan Art

Pearls of Wisdom — *Prayers for Engaged Living*

Sutra of the Medicine Buddha

About Buddha's Light Publishing

As long as Venerable Master Hsing Yun has been a Buddhist monk, he has had a strong belief that books and other documentation of the Buddha's teachings unite us emotionally, help us practice Buddhism at a higher level, and continuously challenge our views on how we define our lives.

In 1996, the Fo Guang Shan International Translation Center was established with this goal in mind. This marked the beginning of a string of publications translated into various languages from the Master's original writings in Chinese. Presently, several translation centers have been set up worldwide. Centers that coordinate translation or publication projects are located in Los Angeles and San Diego, USA; Sydney, Australia; Berlin, Germany; Argentina; South Africa; and Japan.

In 2001, Buddha's Light Publishing was established to publish Buddhist books translated by the Fo Guang Shan International Translation Center as well as other valuable Buddhist works. Buddha's Light Publishing is committed to building bridges between East and West, Buddhist communities, and cultures. All proceeds from our book sales support Buddhist propagation efforts.